3

P1

2

01

4

6 5

6

7

8 7

E1

10

11

12

10 13

G1

L1

14

G2

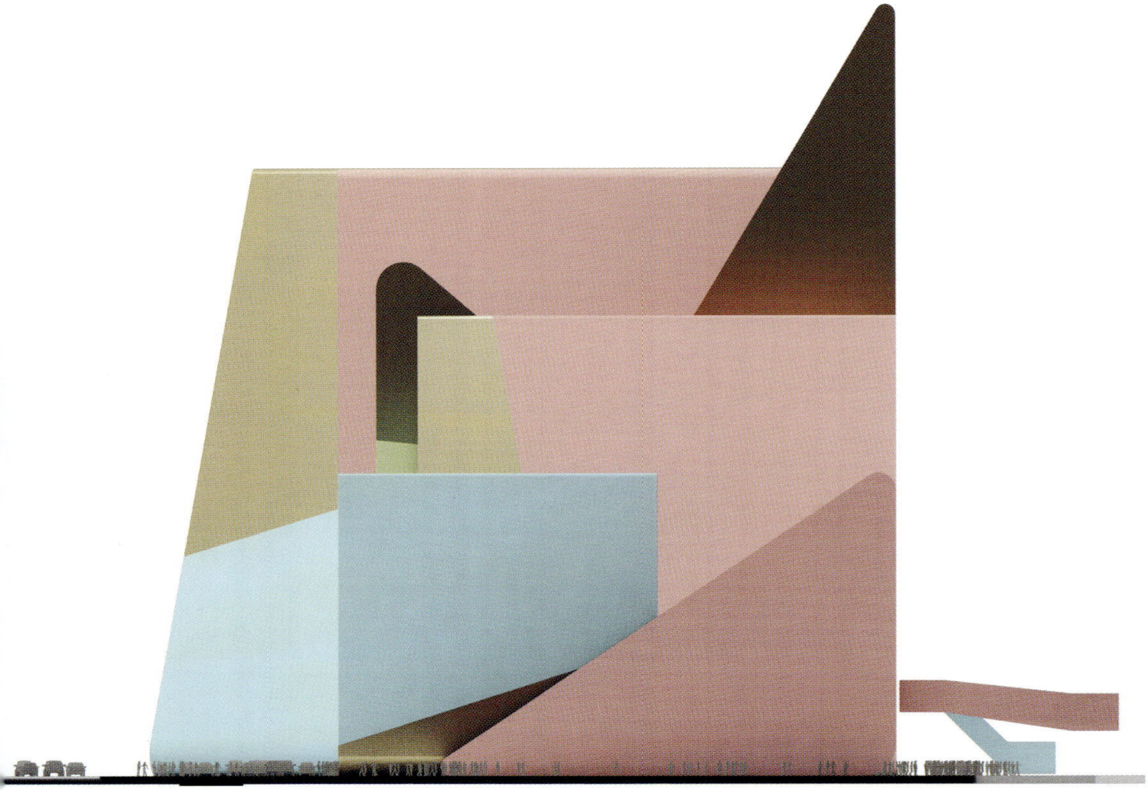

P2

K1

E4

F2

18

15

M1

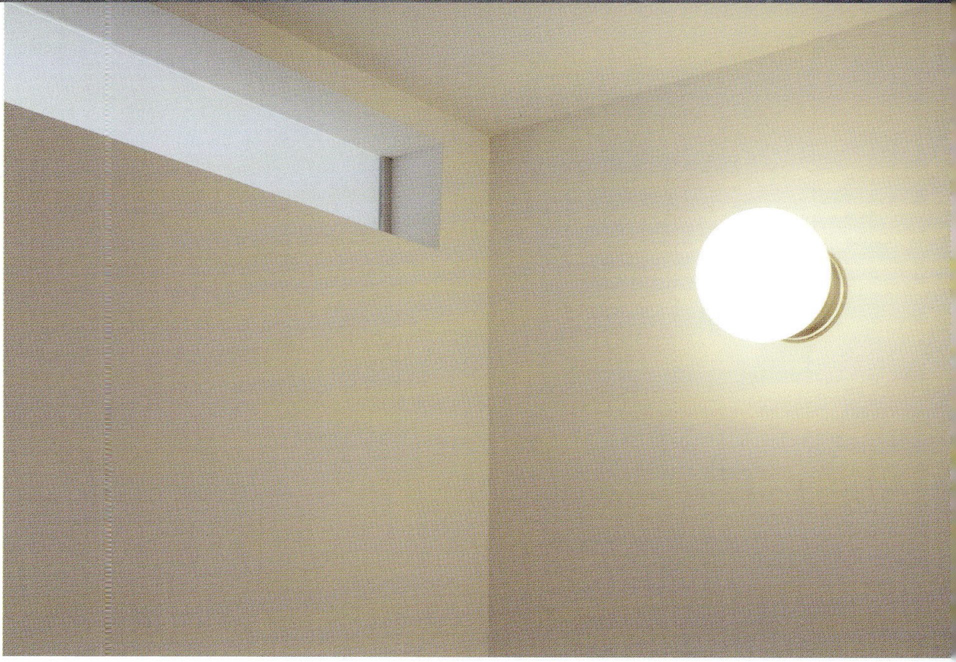

O3

16

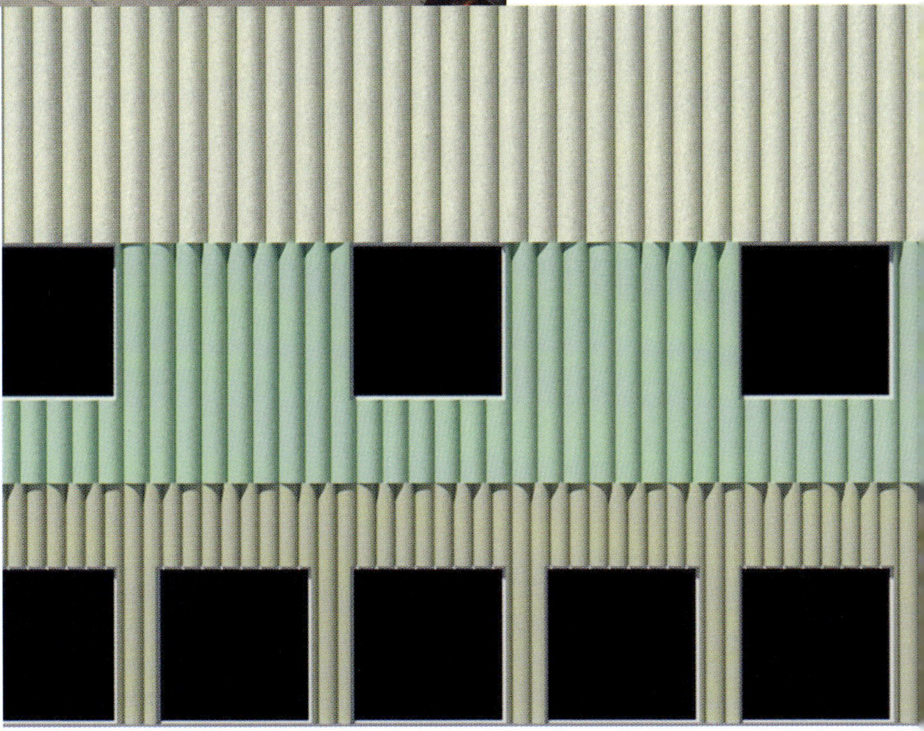

C1

17

18

L2

19

B1

L3

21

G3

C2

22

M3

 23

K2

24

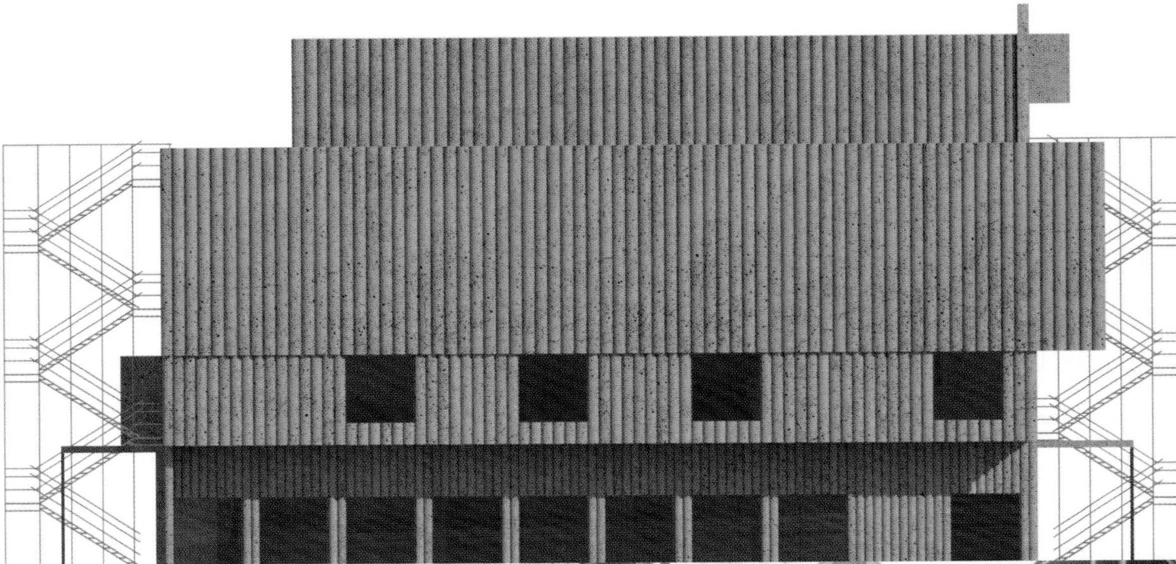

C3

ALFRED R. PREISSNER
PLUMBING
2531 W. DIVISION ST.
HUMBOLDT 6-1958

25

26

F3

K3

M4

27

28

29

34

E5

N1

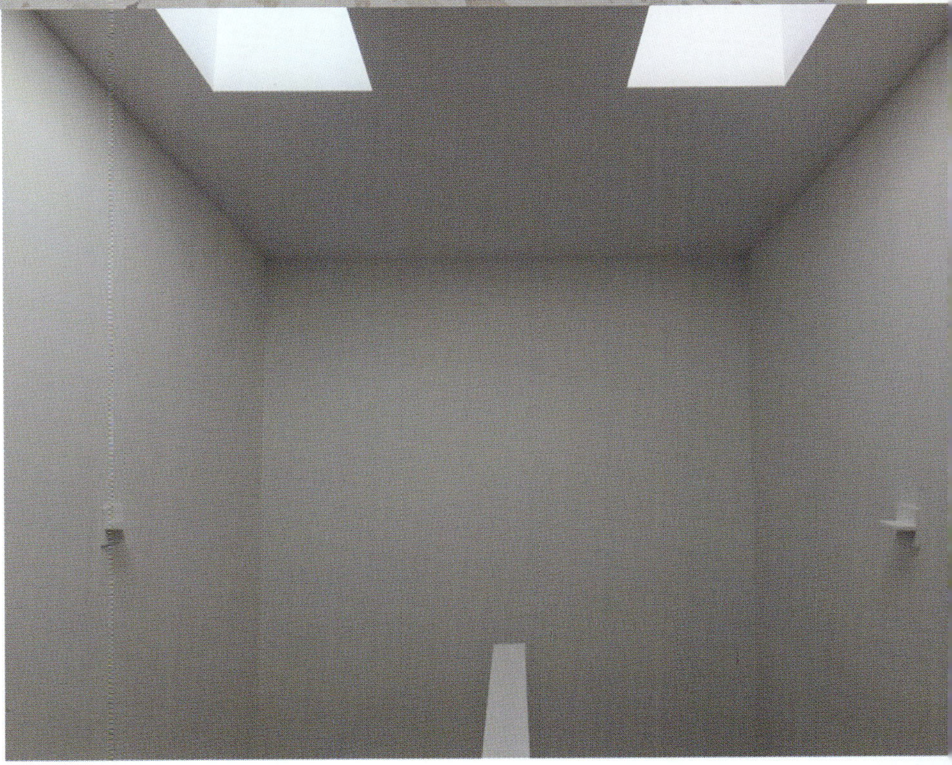

E6

30

31

32

K4

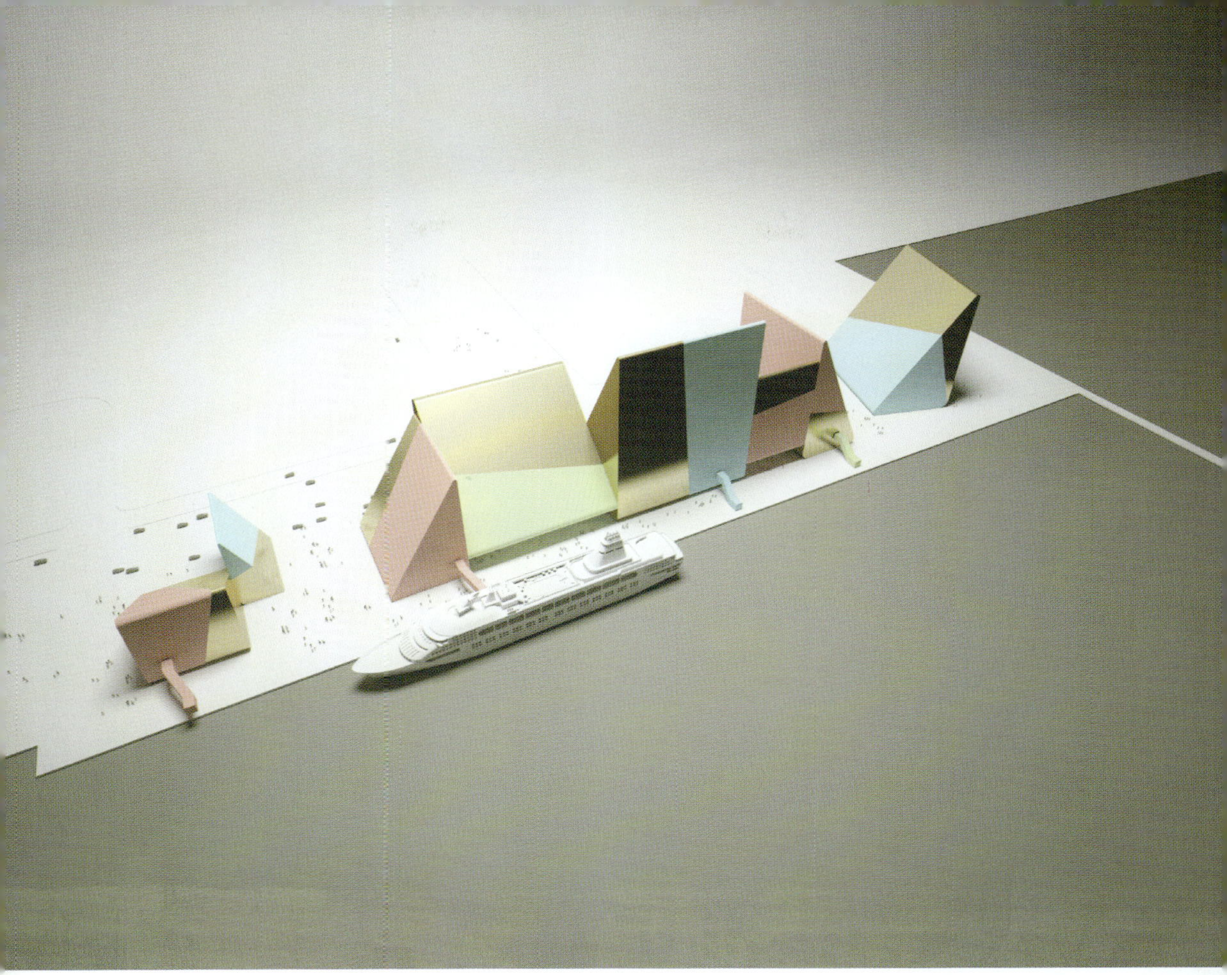

P3

33

L4

A1

C4

J1

A2

C5

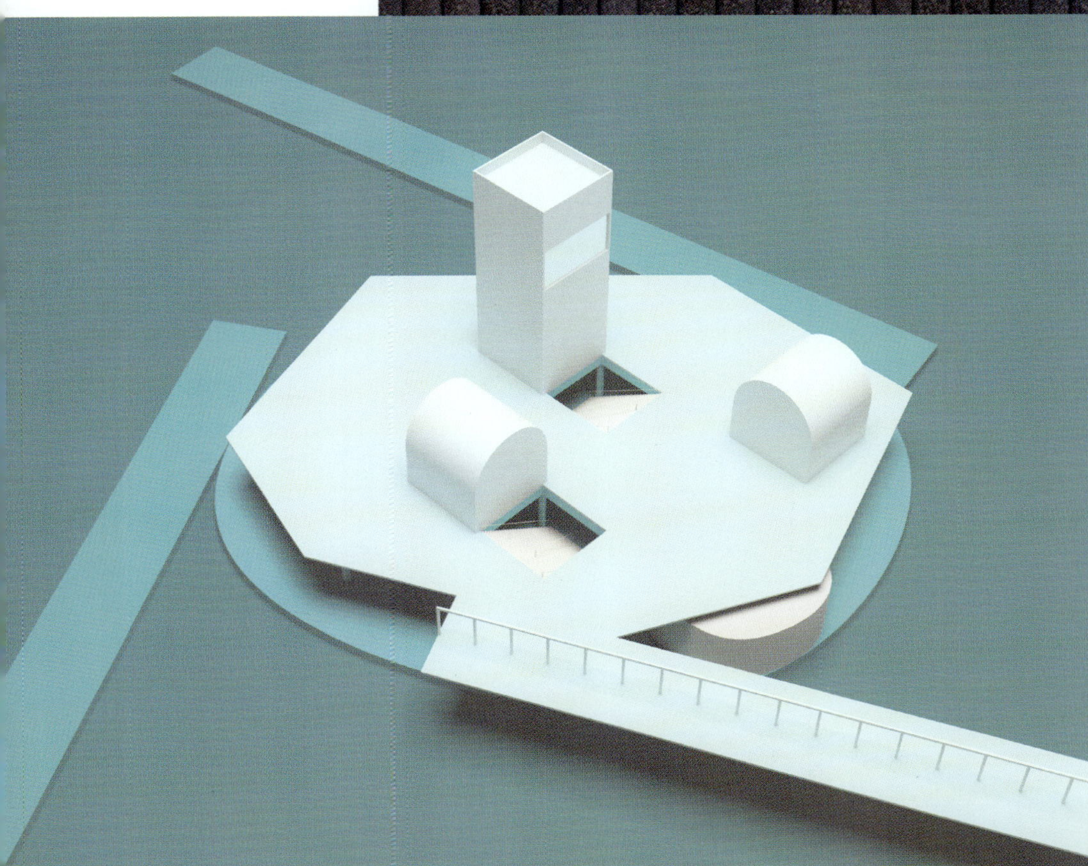

35

C6

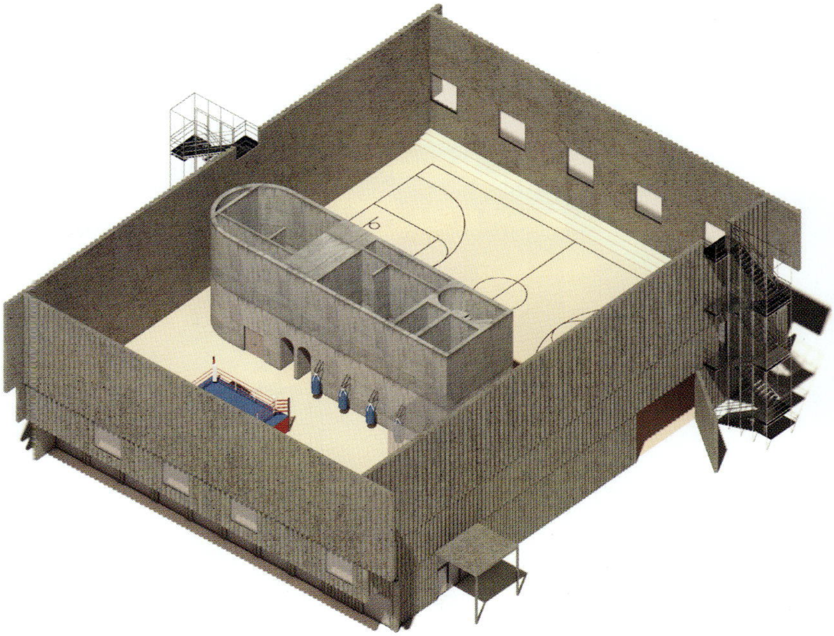

L5

A3

36

37

38

E7

 39

N2

40

E8

50 41

I1

42

K6

P4

43

M4

J2

54

44

1824 — 22

Kind of Boring
Canonical Work and Other Visible Things Meant to be Viewed as Architecture

Paul Preissner

Essays by
Jayne Kelley
Alex Lehnerer
Walter Benn Michaels
Li Tavor

Edited by
Courtney Coffman

Text Drawings by
Tim Kinsella

Graphic Design by
Joe Gilmore

Typeface
Favorit by Dinamo

Printed by
Arlequin, Barcelona

Contents

Projects

&____&
&_LILiLIL/LILI&=Li7ILI7ILILI &_7ILILILILILi&=LILILiLILI7I&
&=LILILiLIL/LI&_LILi7ILI7ILI &=LI7ILILILiLI&_LILILILi7ILI&
&_LILILILiLIL/&=LILILi7ILI7I &_LILI7ILiLILI&=LILILI7ILiLI&
&=L/LILILILiLI&_LILILILi7ILI &=LILILi7ILILI&_LILI7ILILILi&
&_LIL/LILILILi&=7ILILILILi7I &_LILiL/LI7ILI&=LI7ILILILiLI&
&=LILIL/LILiLI&_LI7ILI7ILILi &=LiLIL/LILI7I&_7ILILILiLILI&
&_LILILIL/LILI&=LILI7ILI7iLI &_LILiLILI7ILI&=LI7ILiLILILI&
&=LILILiLIL/LI&_LILILI7iLI7I &=LILILi7ILILI&_LILi7ILILILI&
&_LILiLILILIL/&=7ILILiLI7ILI &_L/LI7ILiLILI&=LiLILI7ILILI&
&=LiLILILILILI&_LI7iLILILI7I &=LI7ILIL/LiLI&_LILiLILI7ILI&
&_LILiLIL/LILI&=7iLI7ILILILI &_7IL/LILILILi&=LILILiLILI7I&
&=LILILiLIL/LI&_LI7iLI7IL/LI &=LI7ILILILiLI&_LILILILi7ILI&
&_LILILILiLIL/&=LILI7iLI7ILI &_LILI7ILiLILI&=LILILI7ILiLI&
&=L/LILILILiLI&_LILILI7iL/7I &=LILILi7ILILI&_LILI7ILILILi&
&_LIL/LILILILi&=LILILILI7iLI &_LILiLILI7ILI&=LI7ILILILiLI&
&=LILIL/LILiLI&_7ILILILILI7i &=LiL/LILILI7I&_7ILILILiLILI&

I remember
Lebanon on the news a lot when I was a boy.
And
Communism.
I remember

how much I didn't know about anything and how

much I don't.

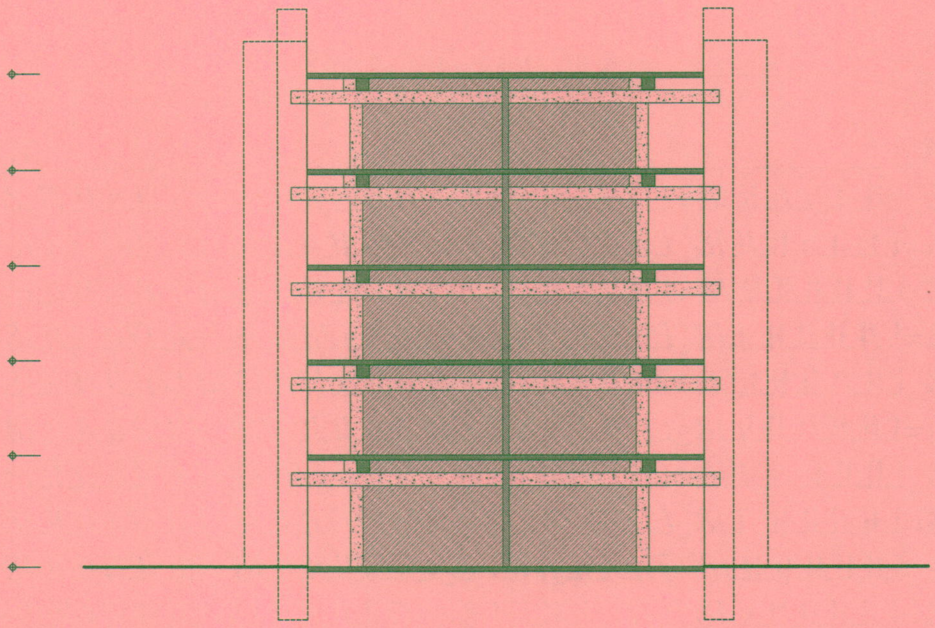

Building 4 Section (E-W)

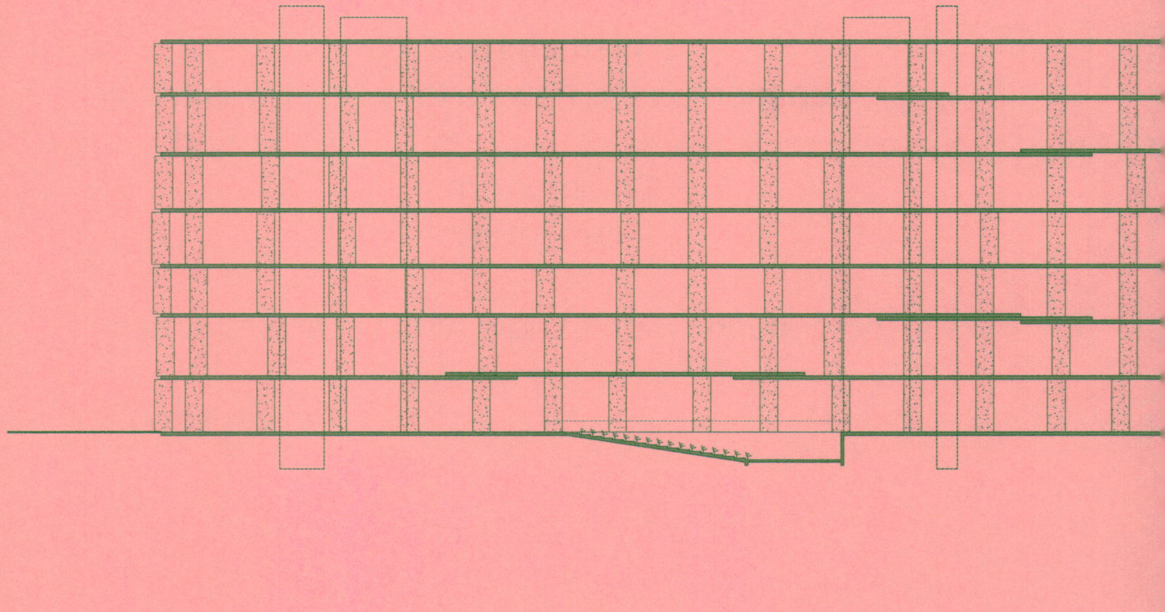

Building 2 Section (N-S)

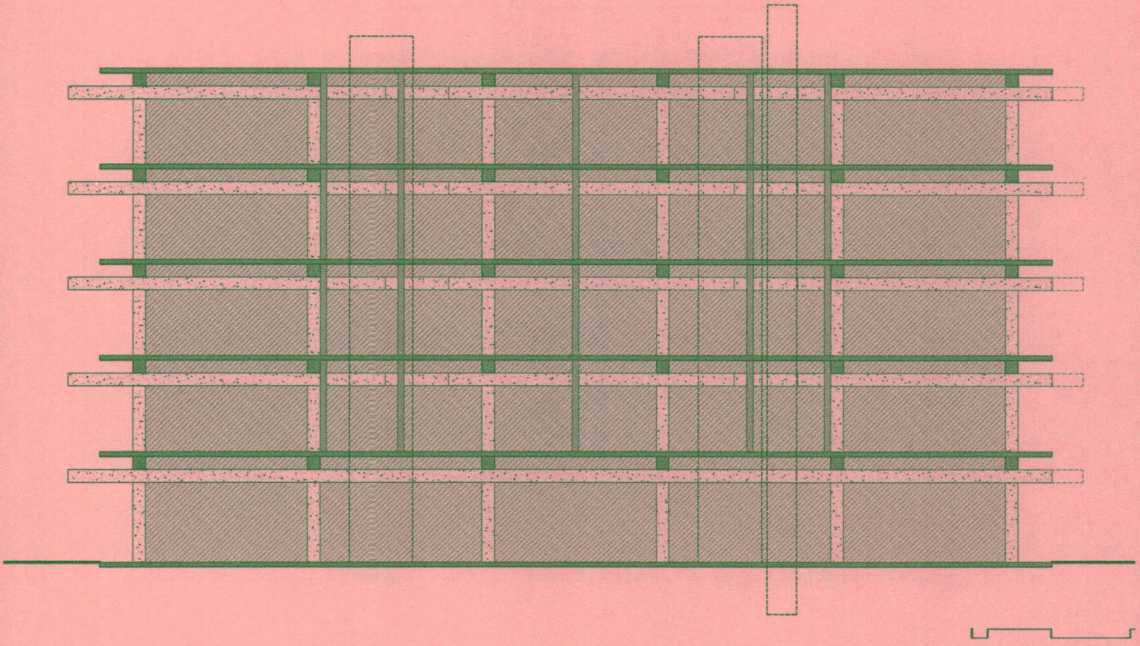

Building 4 Section (N-S)

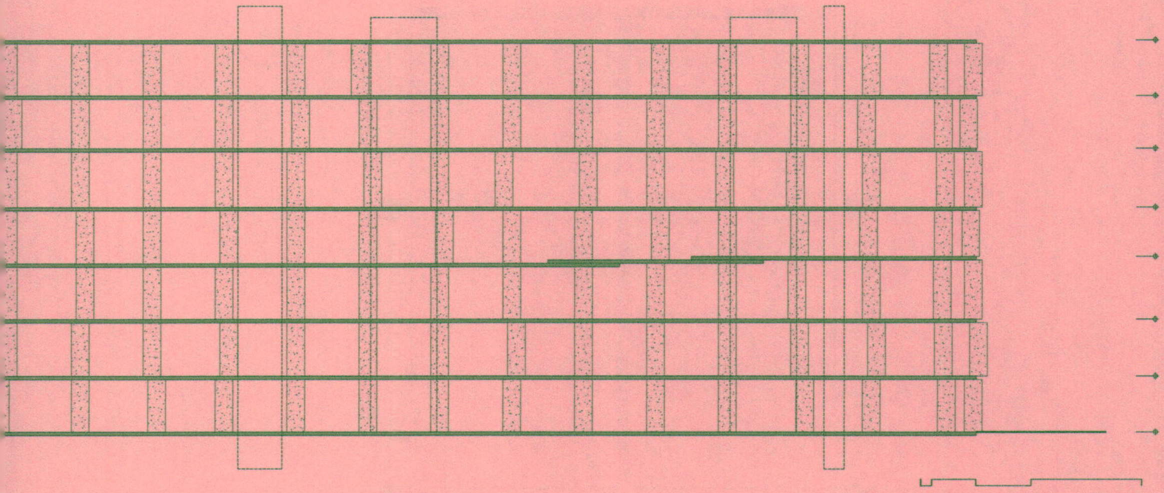

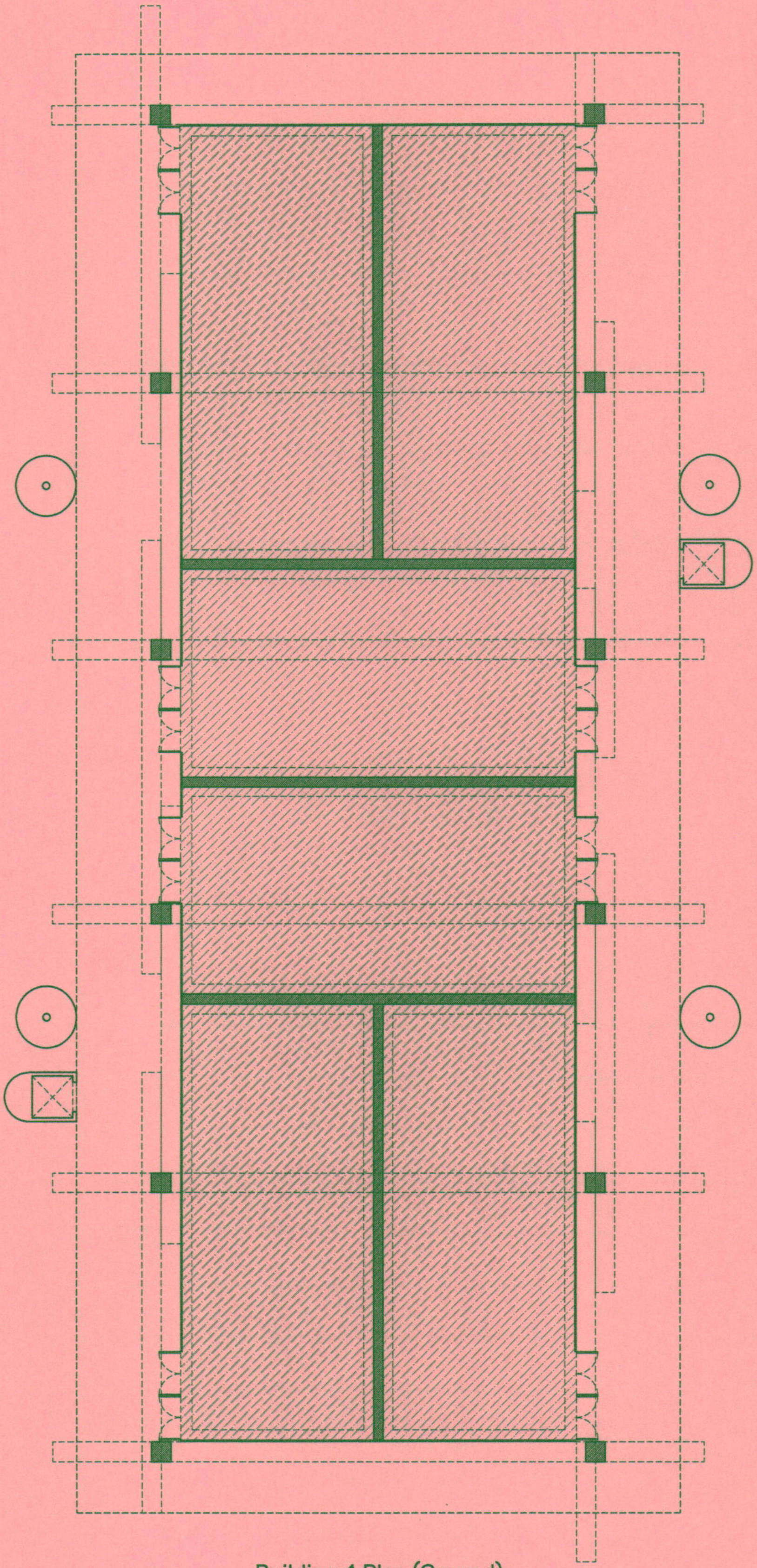

Building 4 Plan (Ground)

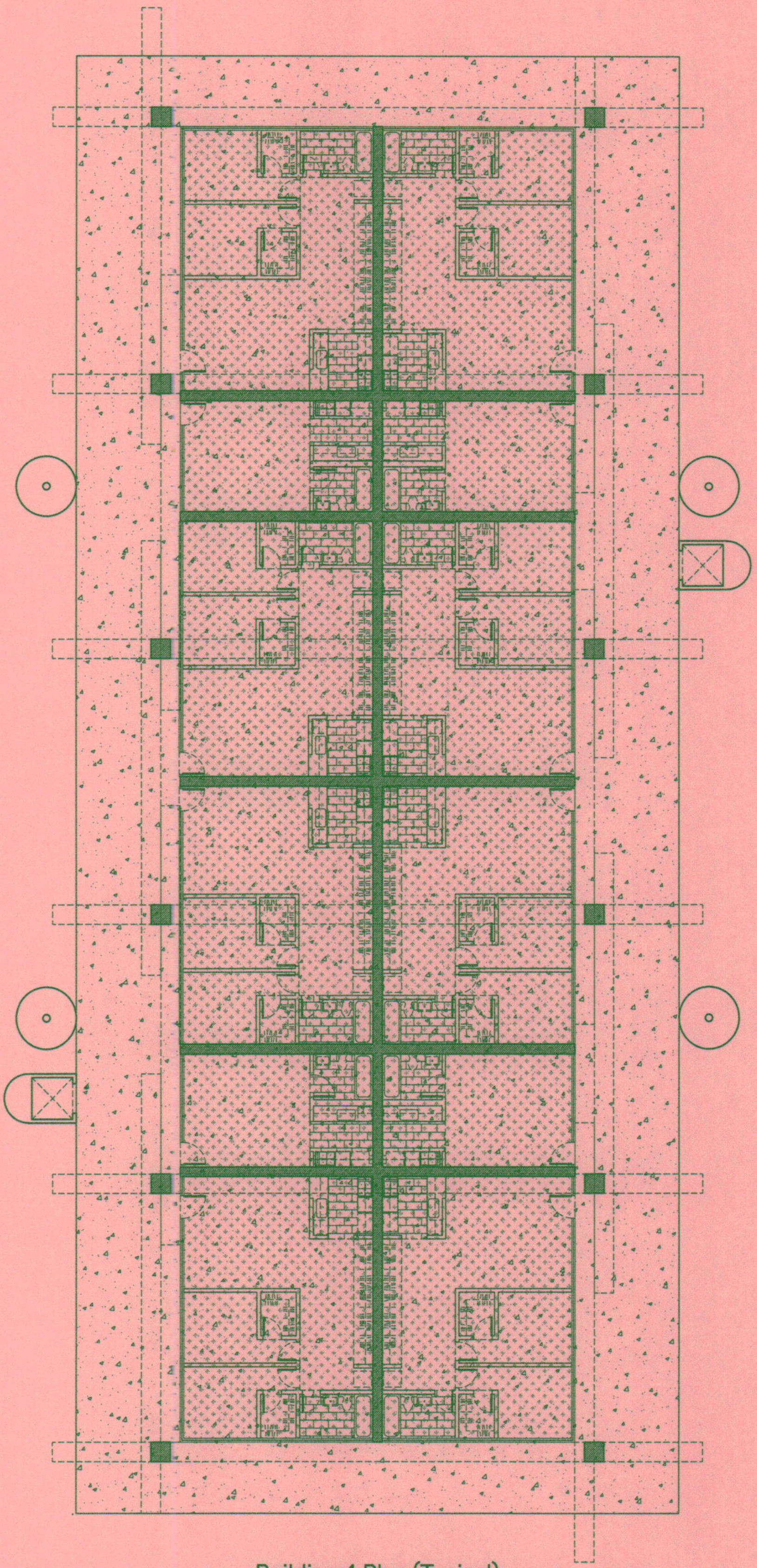

Building 4 Plan (Typical)

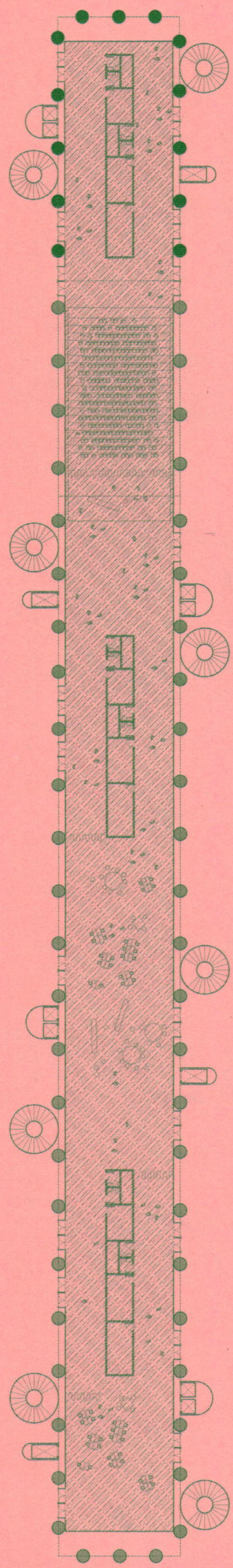

Building 2 Plan (Ground)

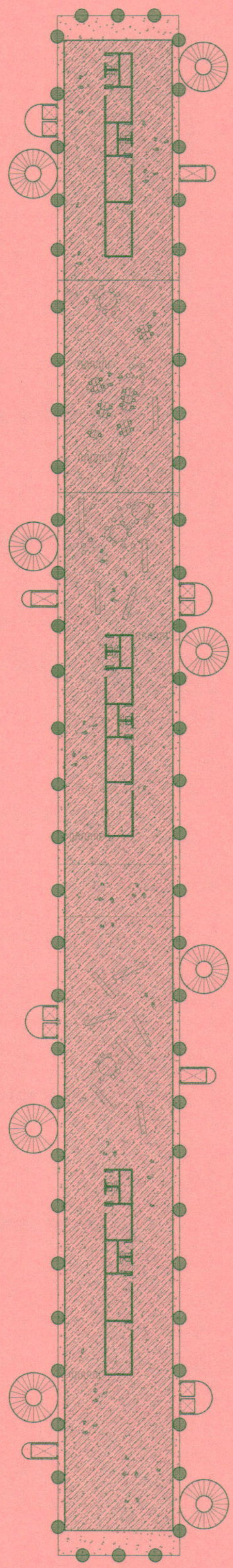

Building 2 Plan (Typical)

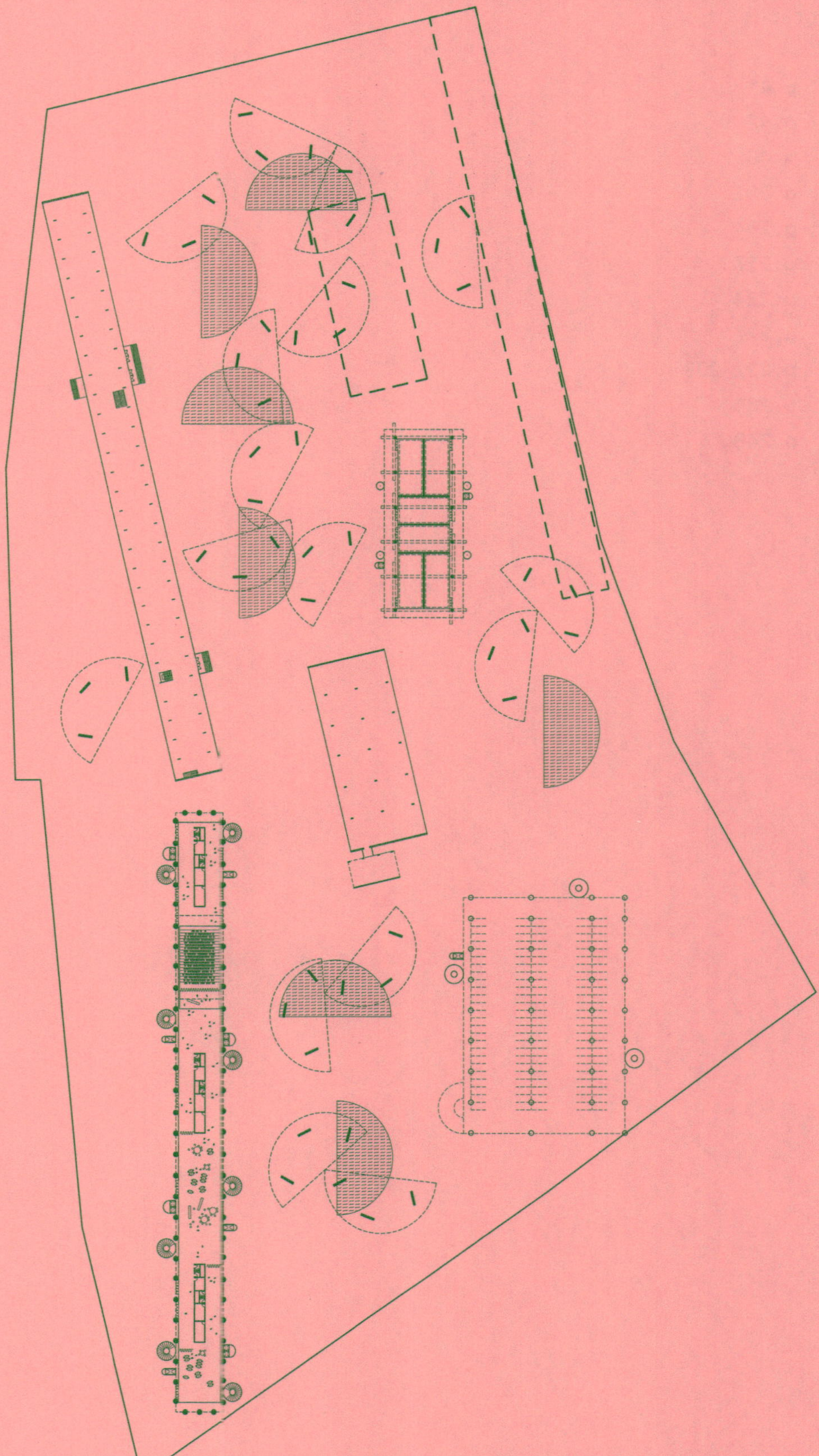

Site Plan

Photographs

WOODS WOODS WOODS WOODS WOODS WOODS WOODS
WOODS WOODS WOODS WOODS WOODS WOODS WOODS
WOODS WOODS WOODS WOODS WOODS WOODS WOODS
WOODS WOODS WOODS WOODS WOODS WOODS WOODS
WOODS WOODS WOODS WOODS WOODS WOODS WOODS
WOODS WOODS WOODS house **WOODS WOODS WOODS**
WOODS WOODS WOODS WOODS WOODS WOODS WOODS
WOODS WOODS WOODS WOODS WOODS WOODS *RIVER*
WOODS WOODS WOODS WOODS WOODS *RIVER* **WOODS**
WOODS WOODS WOODS WOODS *RIVER* **WOODS WOODS**
WOODS WOODS WOODS *RIVER* **WOODS WOODS WOODS**

window/door window/door window/door window/door
door/window door/window door/window door/window
window/door window/door window/door window/door

bedroom bedroom

All the pieces laid out simply and correctly with intent make the whole what it is.
Especially in relative isolation this is evident.

And when no one's home, maybe all those animals all play hide and seek together: deer, coyote, rabbits, foxes.

That's what you think animals do when people aren't looking?

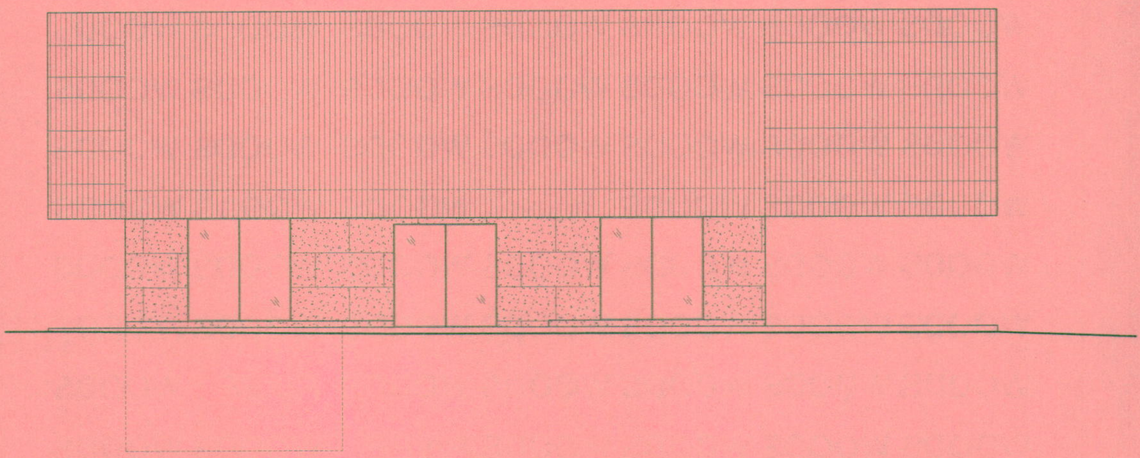

Elevation (East)

Elevation (North)

Elevation (South)

Elevation (West)

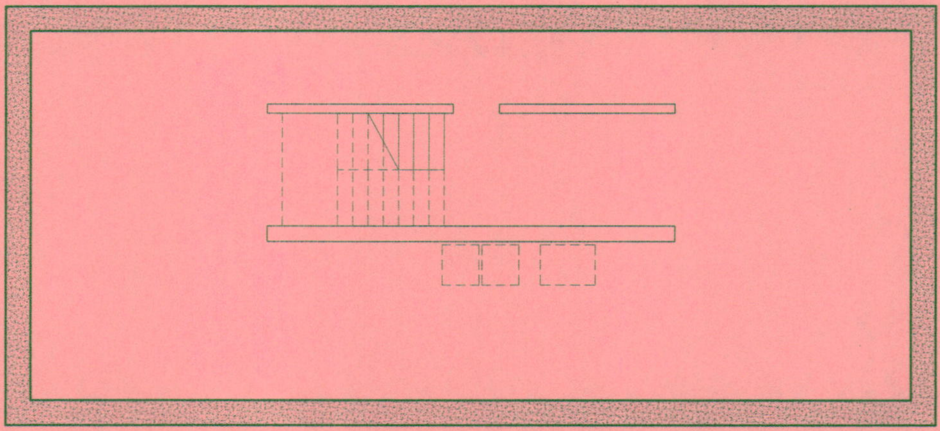

Plan (Basement)

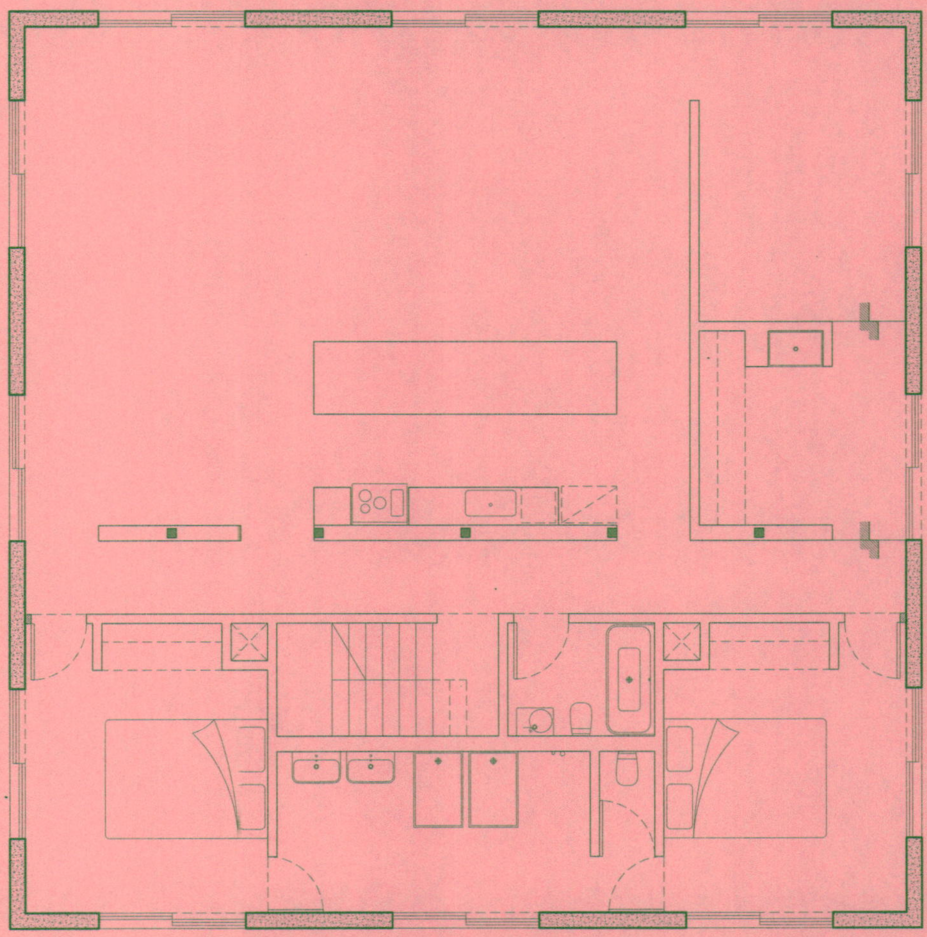

Plan (Ground)

Photographs

B1 p.23
B2 p.213
B3 p.241

road T I

T road T N road

R road R T road

A road A E road

I road I Road

N road N road S

T road T road T

road road road roəd road road Road Road road roAd road road road

HOPE

road roAd A T

road road C C E

road road K K

road road S S

road road

road road

(HOPE)

boxing cooking eating

learning training exhibition social

accommodation fitness competition gardening meditation

Have you seen how you can see everything from here? Like how all of it, inside and out, is one long folding continuity doubling back on its own self-aware edges? It’s in the neighborhood in the city in the county in the state in the country in the continent in the world in the solar system in the galaxy in the infiniverse . . .

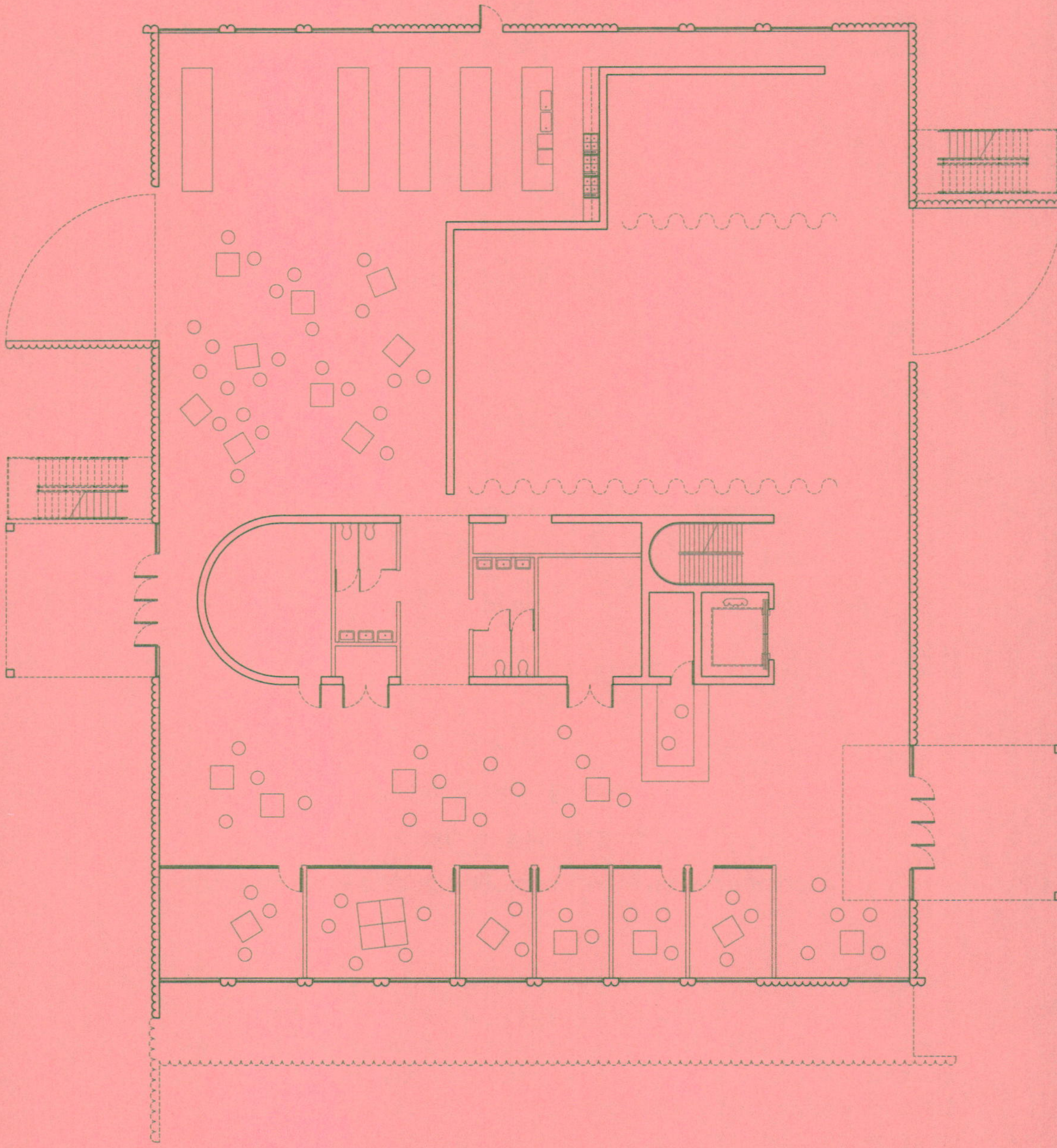

Plan (Ground)

Plan (Upper)

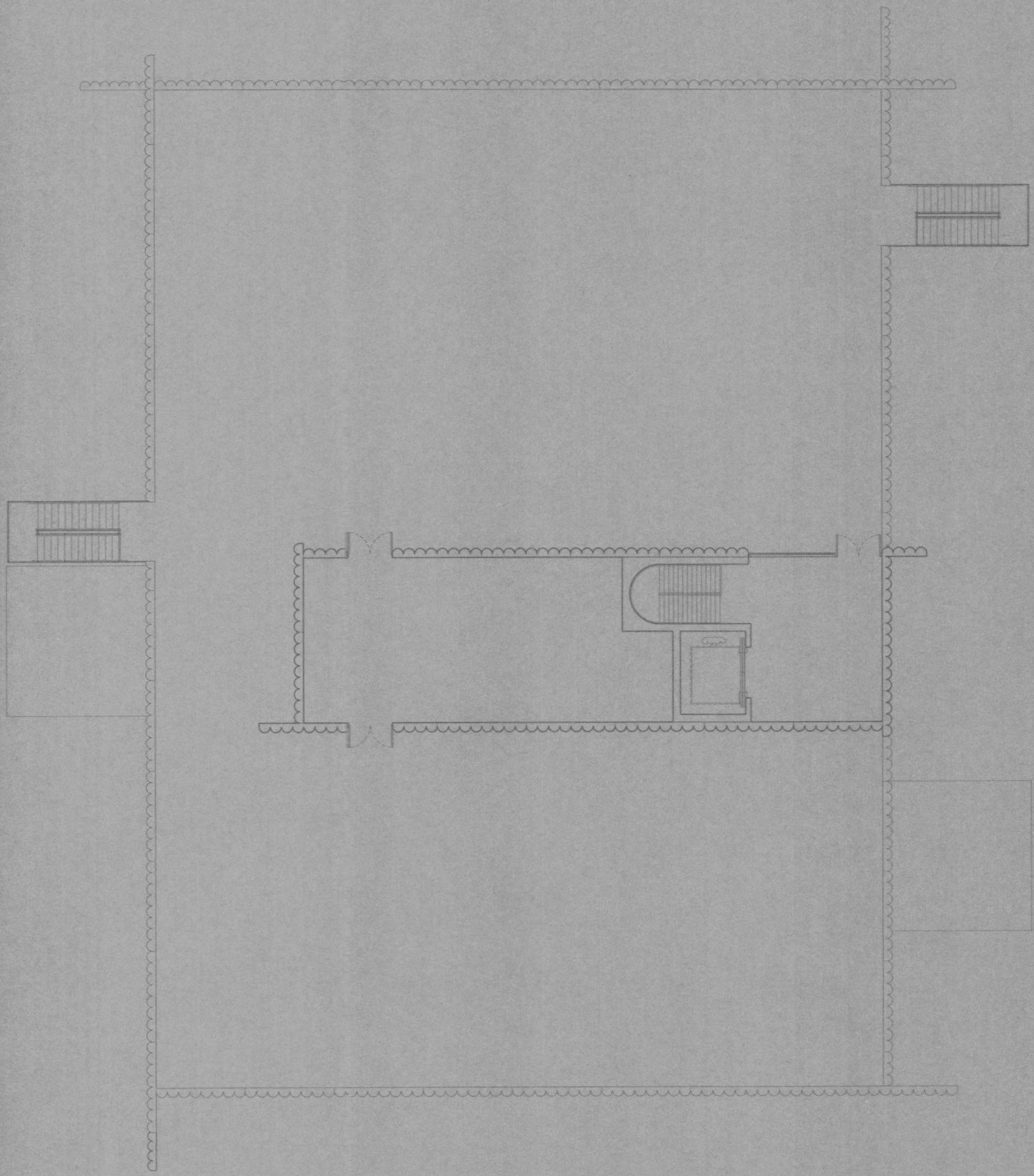

Plan (Roof)

Photographs

EDUCATION MEETING PRAYER––

L L L
I I I
G G G
H H H
T T

----------------->

xx book xx book xx book xx book xx
book xx book xx book xx book xx
book xx book xx book xx book xx
book xx book xx book xx book xx
book xx book xx book xx book xx
book xx book xx book xx book xx
book xx book xx book xx book xx
book xx book xx book xx book xx
book xx book xx book xx book ––––
LECTURE EXHIBIT YOUTH

––PRAYER MEETING EDUCATION

L L L
I I I
G G G
H H H
T T T

<-----------------

xy book xy book xy book xy book xy
book xy book xy book xy book xy
book xy book xy book xy book xy
book xy book xy book xy book xy
book xy book xy book xy book xy
book xy book xy book xy book xy
book xy book xy book xy book xy
book xy book xy book xy book xy
book xy book xy book xy book
YOUTH EXHIBIT LECTURE––––

a mess of shading elements

creates a garden in the desert

Arrange the semicircles in a way so that—in relation to the strange angles cf the lawn and against each other—*these semicircles together become a simple chaos.*

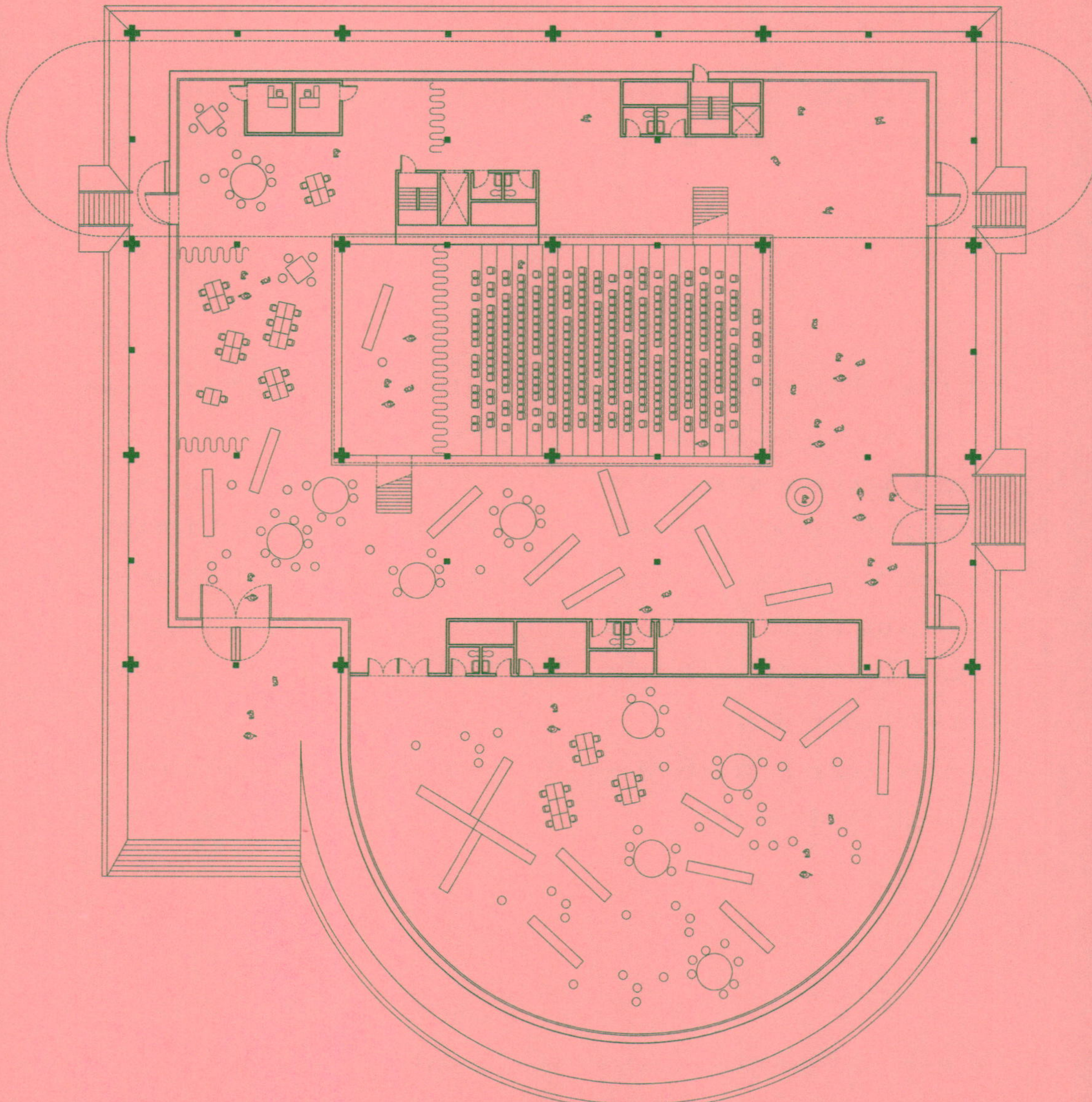

Plan (Ground)

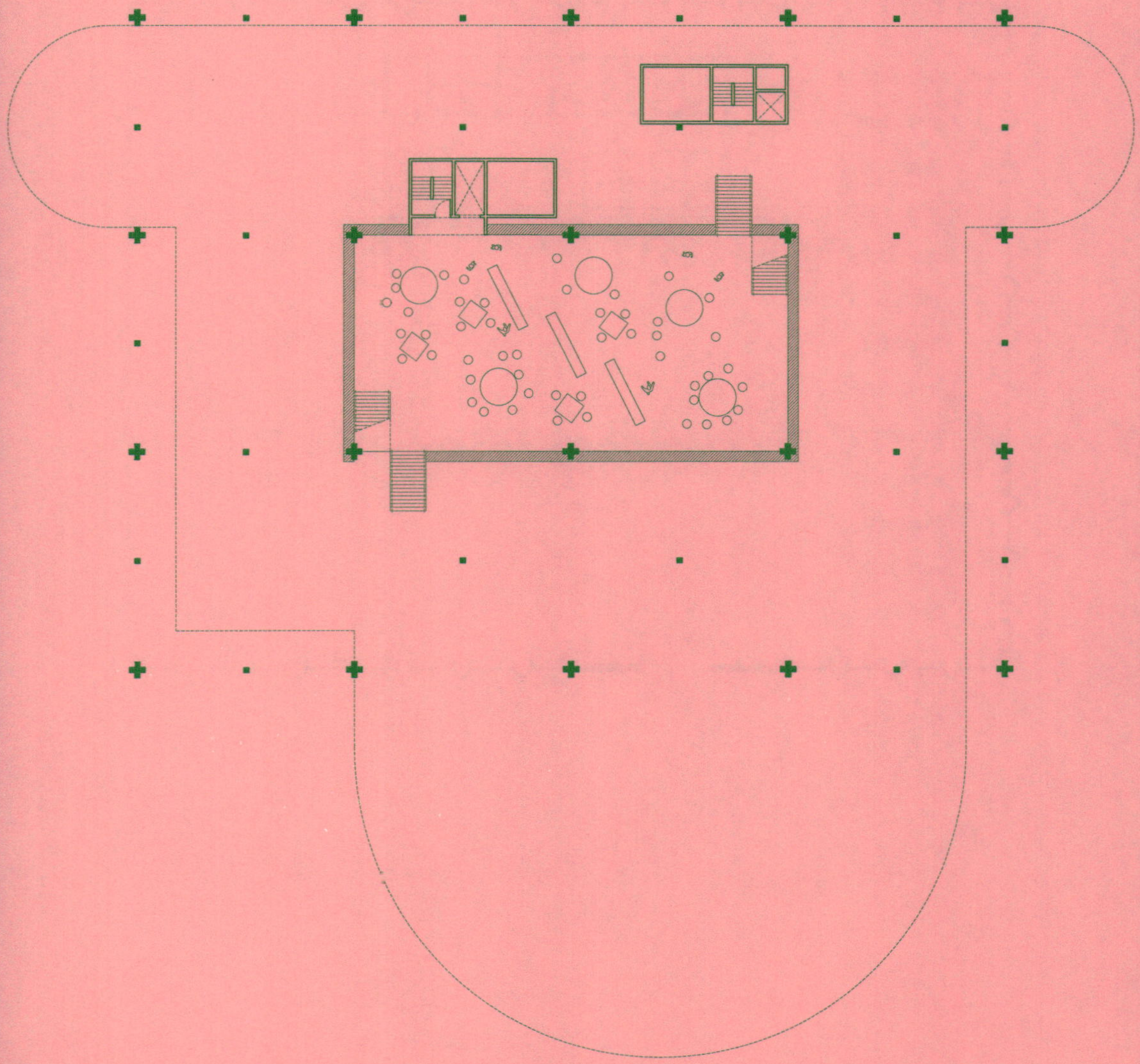

Plan (Mezzanine)

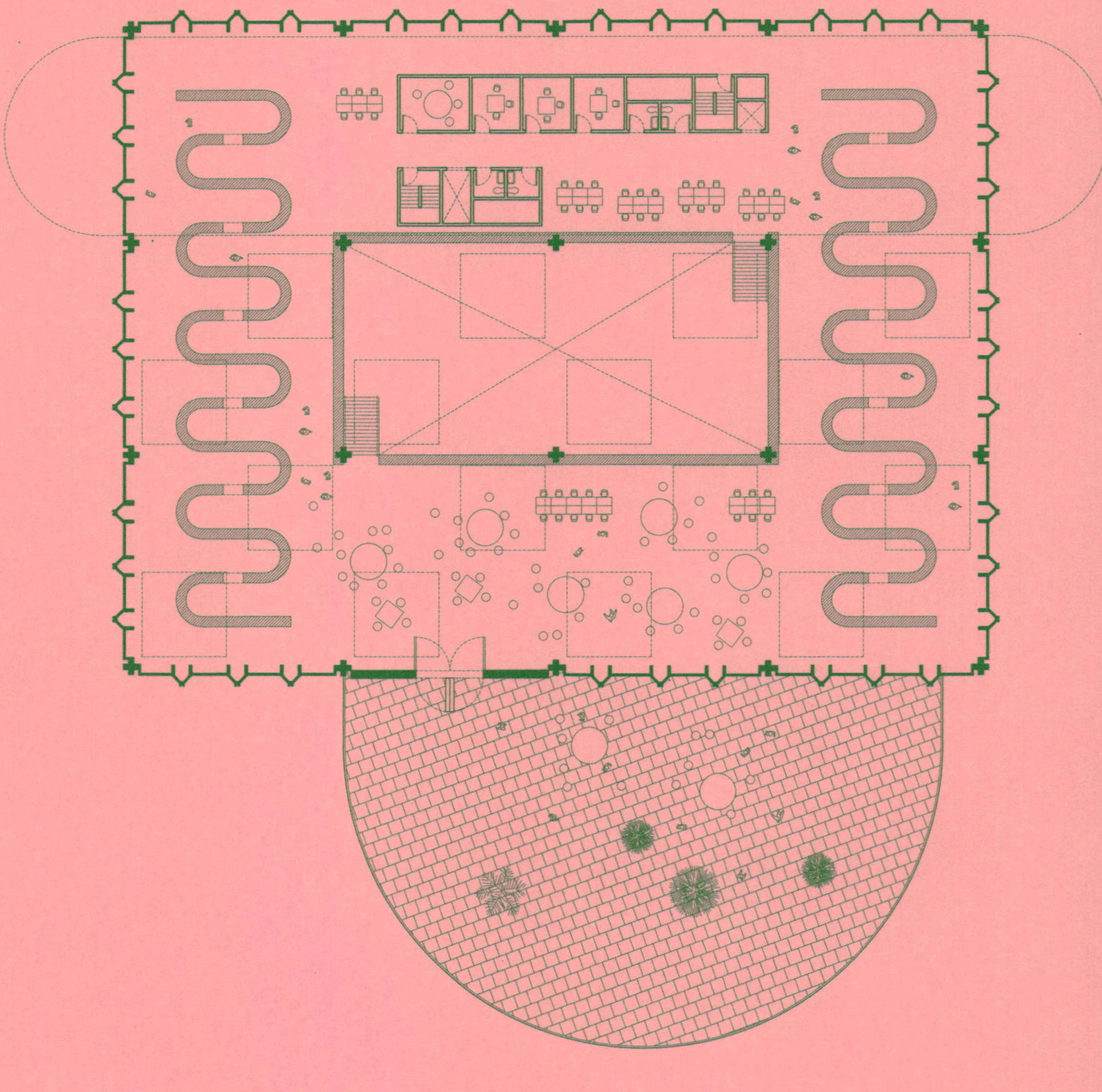

Plan (Level 1)

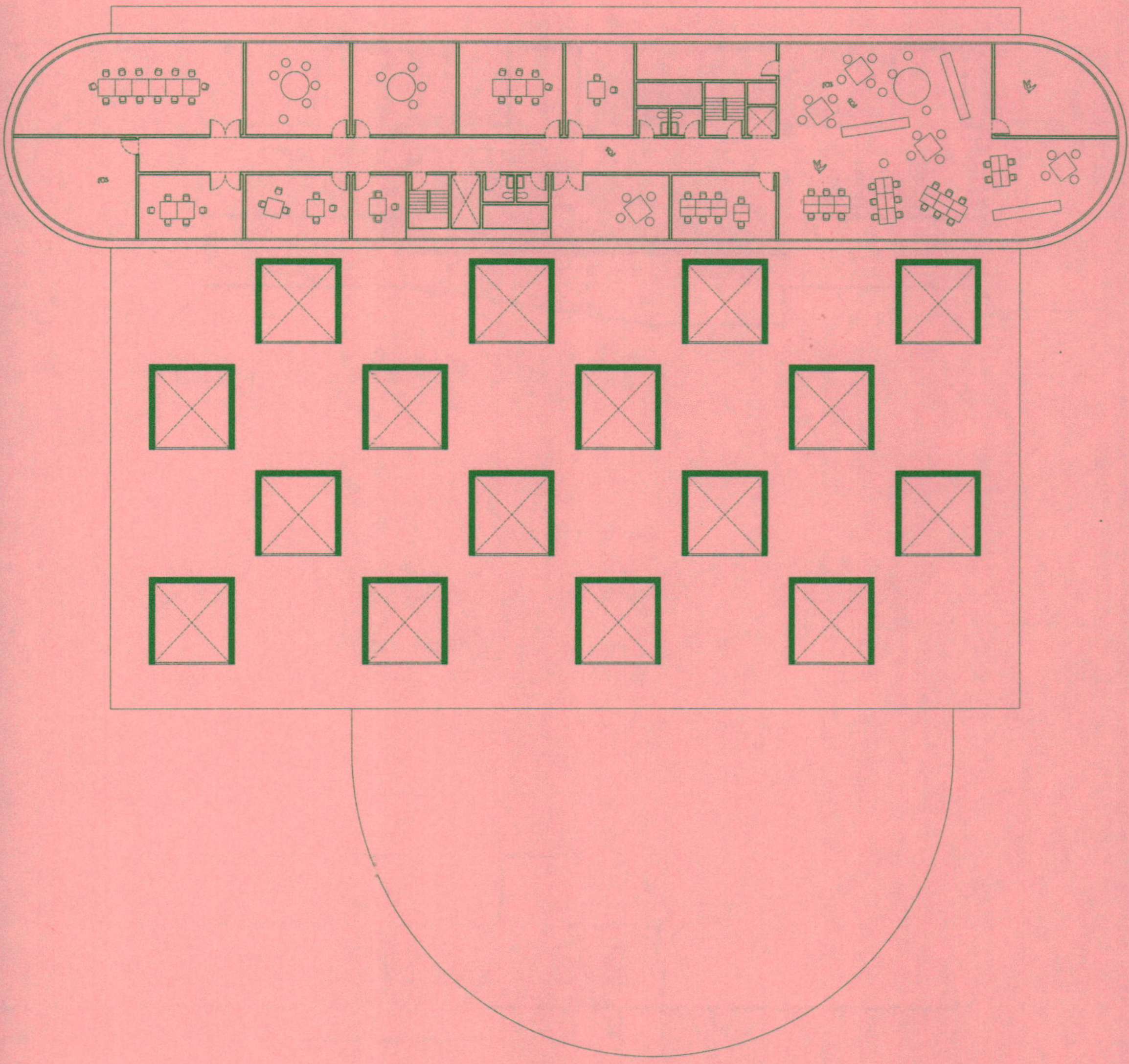

Plan (Level 2)

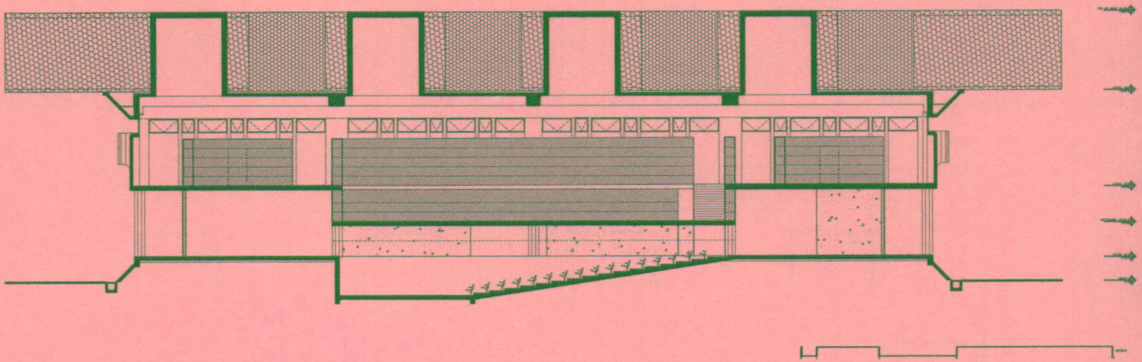

Section (N-S)

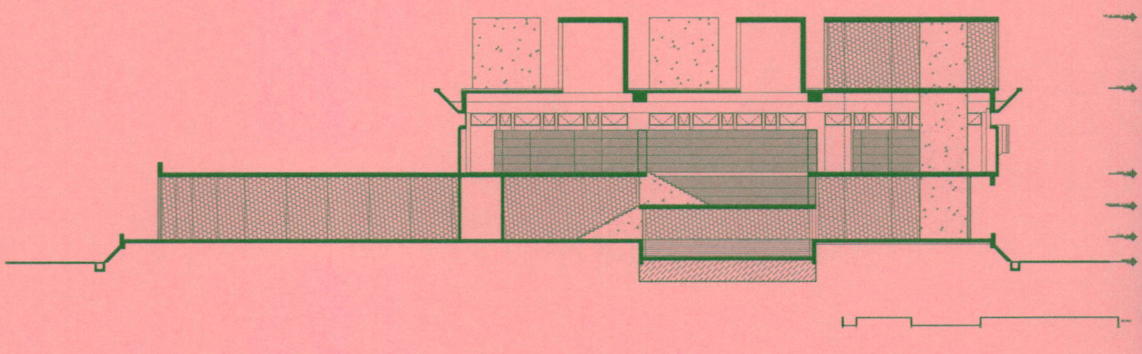

Section (E-W)

Site Plan

Dar Al-Uloum Library

Photographs

the roof is sloped slightly

the roof is sloped slightly

the roof is sloped slightly

LIZ & MORRIS LIVE HERE. SIX OF THEM. BETWEEN THE RIVER AND THE CITY

LIMITS. ALL WHITE BEHIND A PARTIAL COVER OF CHARRED WOOD.

LIZ & MORRIS LIVE HERE. SIX OF THEM. BETWEEN THE RIVER AND THE CITY

LIMITS. ALL WHITE ....CHARRED WOOD.

LIZ & MORRIS LIVE HER..............................WEEN THE RIVER

AND THE CITY LIMITS. A..............................ARTIAL COVER O

.... BETWEEN

THE RIVER AND THE CITY LIMITS. ALL WHITE BEHIN

We see into intertwined symmetries; how each element works and how they all work together. How the light falls on a family. And how we frame our neighbors.

Elevation (East)

Elevation (North)

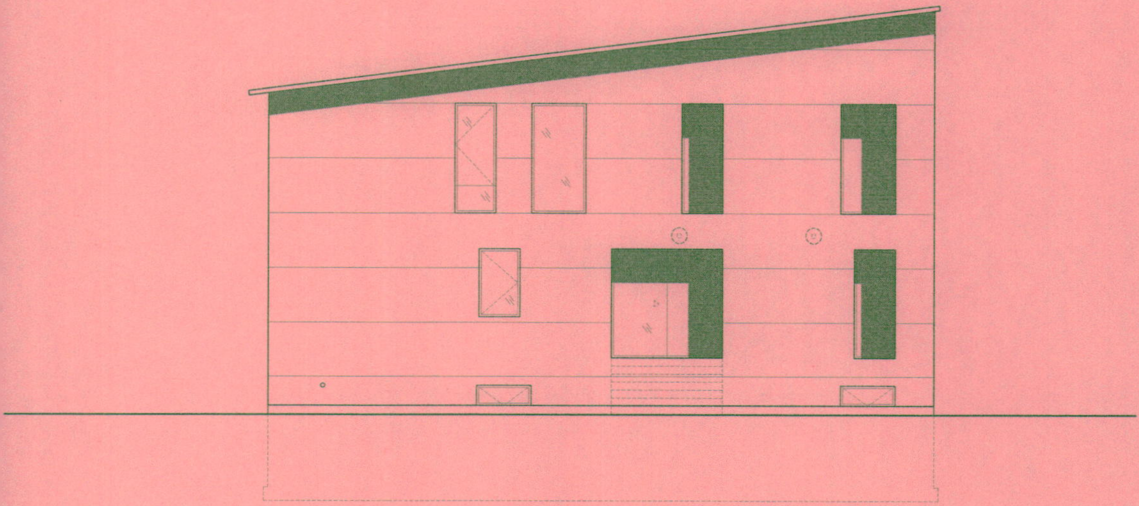

Elevation (South)

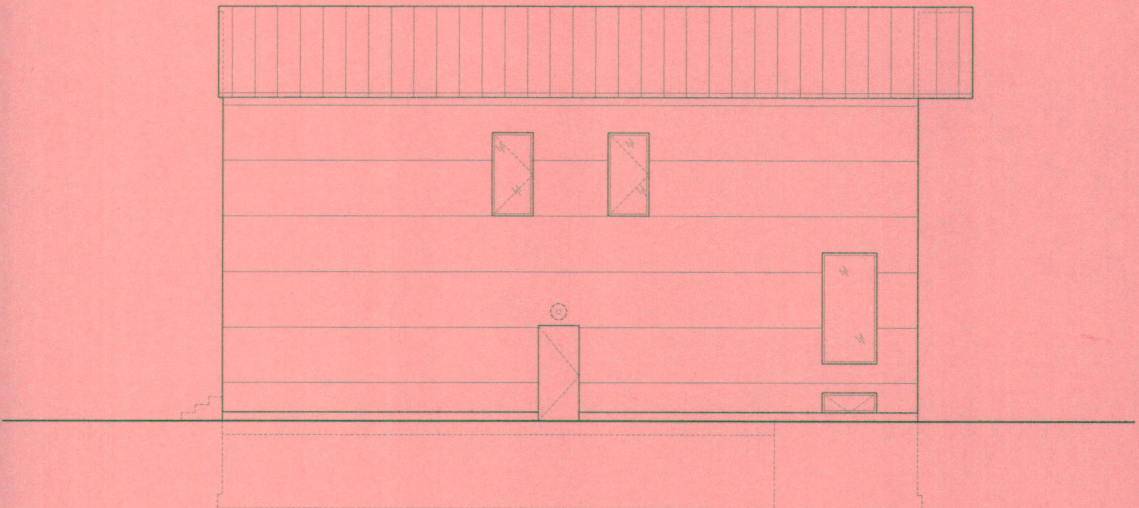

Elevation (West)

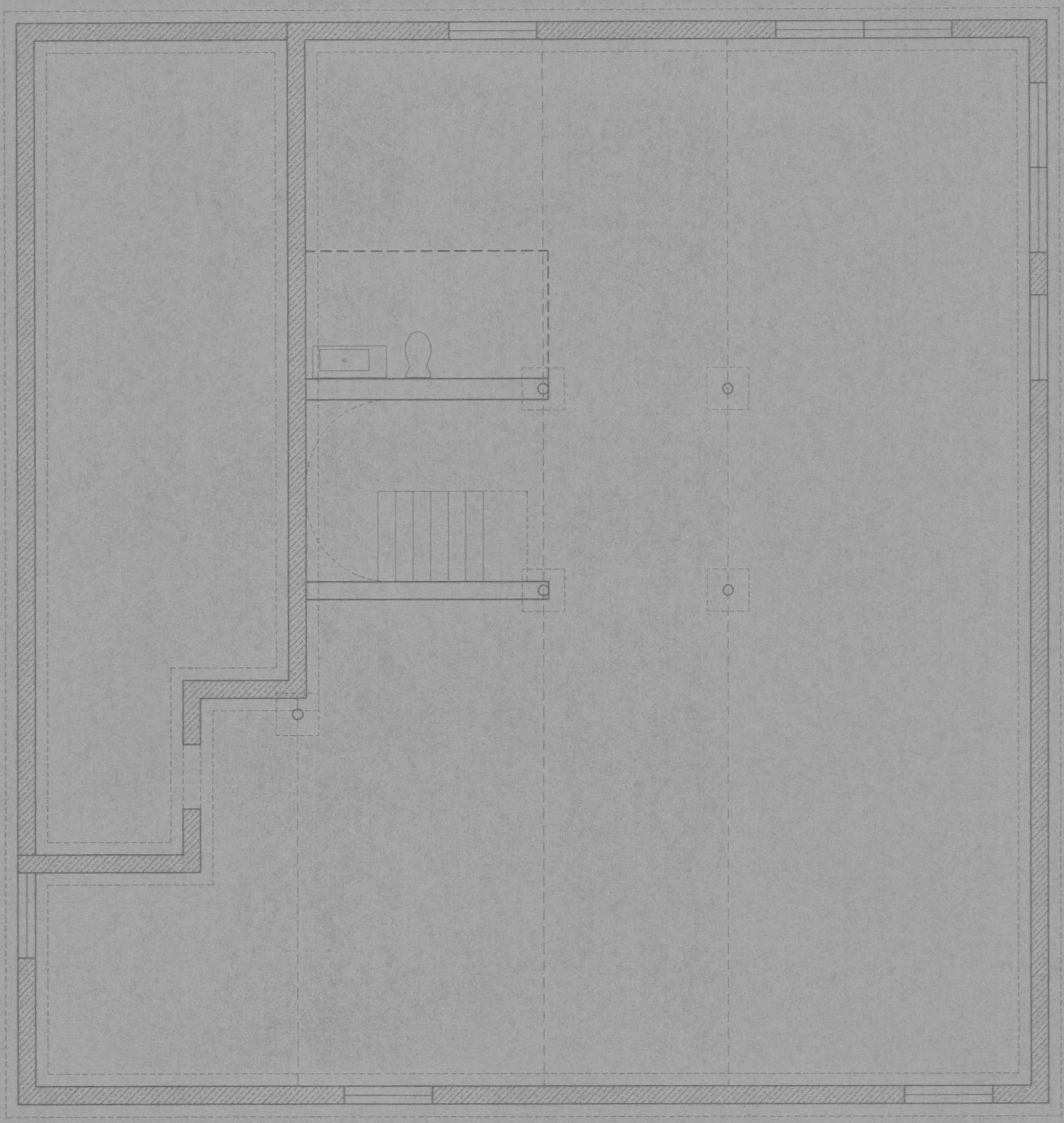

Plan (Basement)

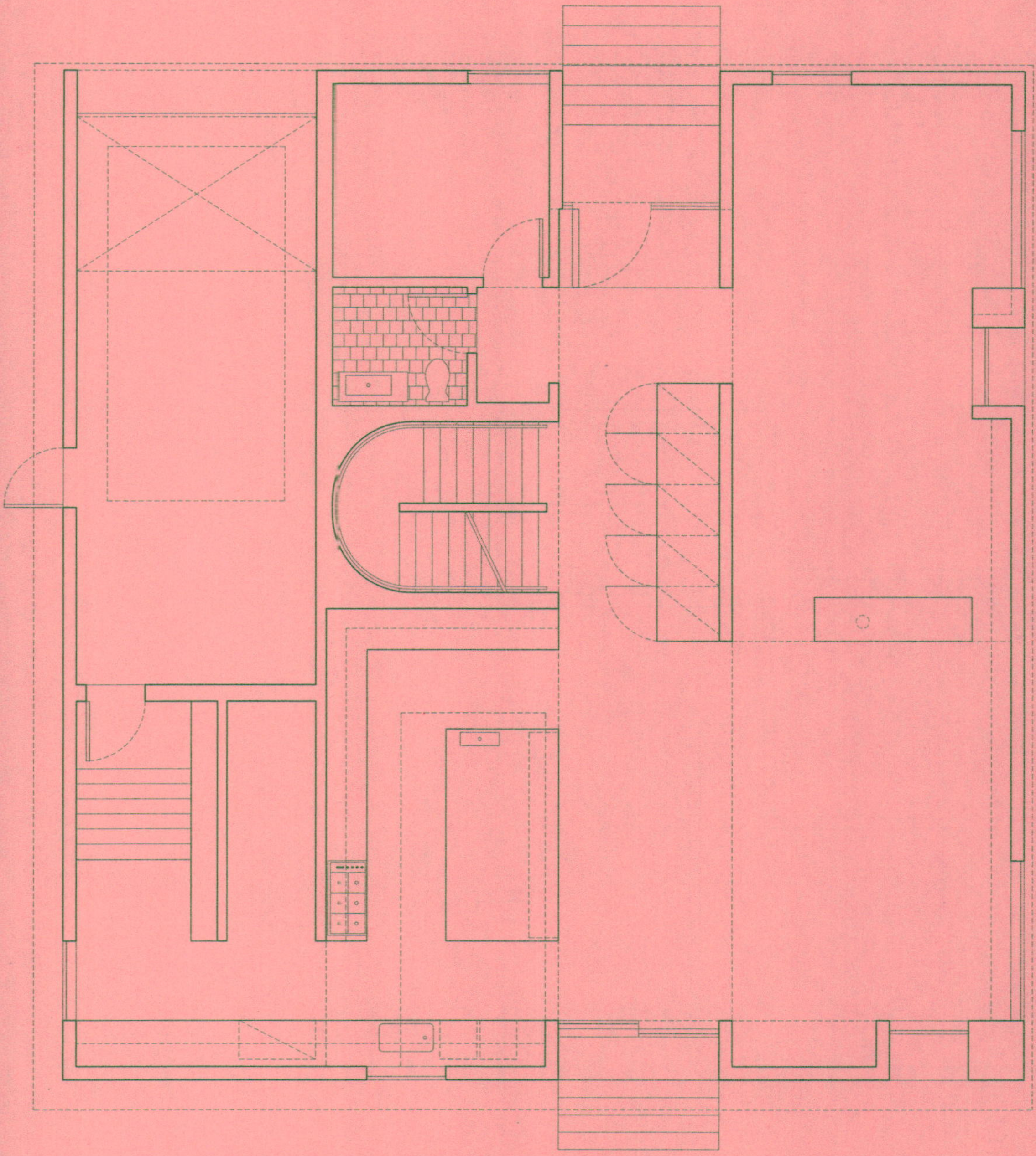

Plan (Ground)

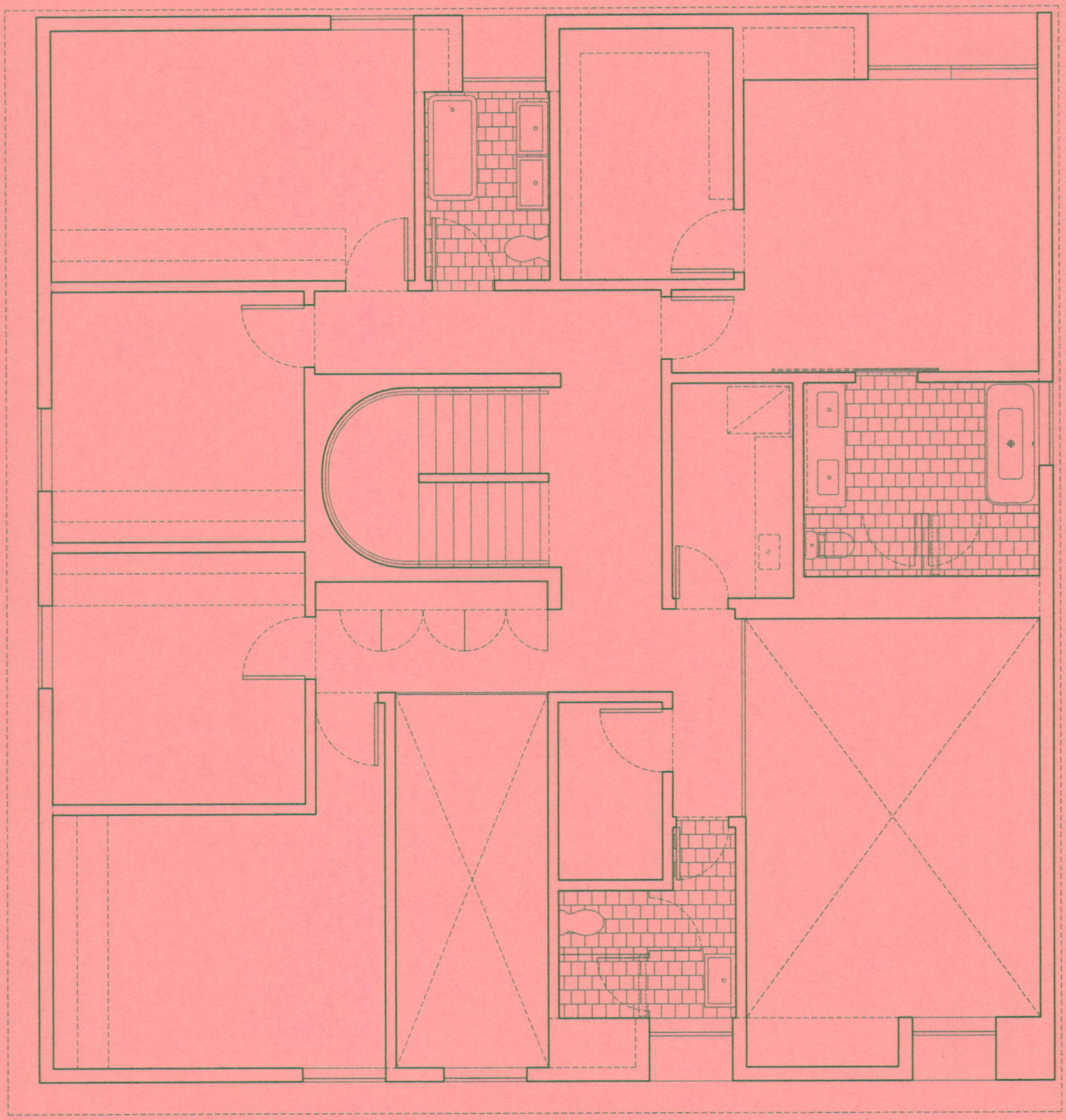

Plan (Upper)

Plan (Roof)

Section 1 (E-W)

Section 2 (E-W)

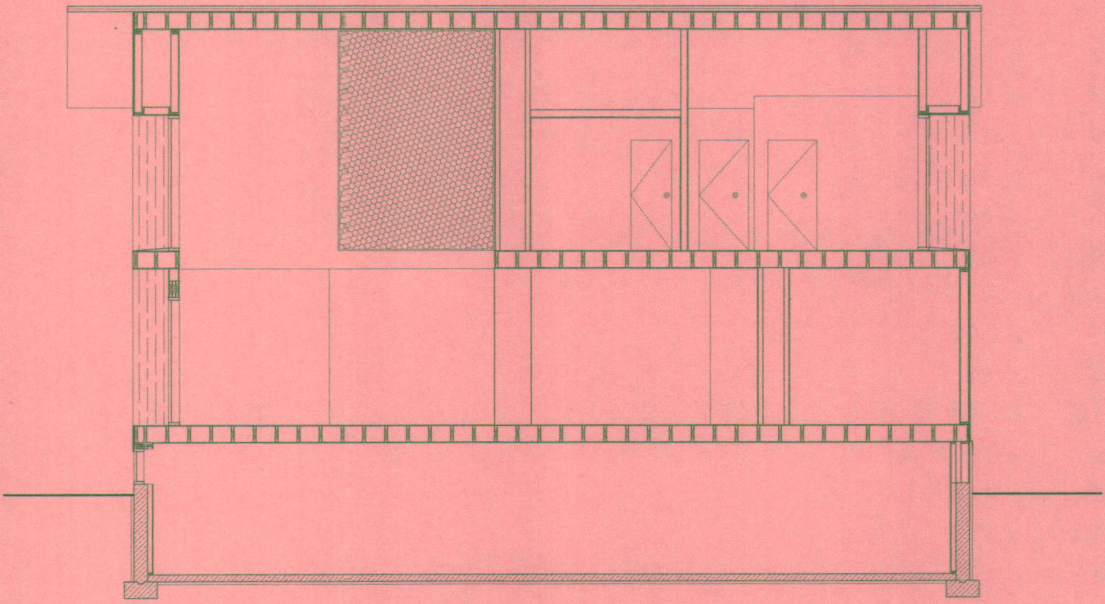

Section 3 (N-S)

Photographs

\\\new windows in deep steel boxes/// \\\new windows in deep steel boxes///

;:;BRICK;:;BRICK;:;BRICK;:;BRICK;:;BRICK;:;BRICK;:;BRICK;:;BRICK;:;BRICK;:;

ICK;:;BRICK;:;BRICK;:;BRICK;:;BRICK;:;BRICK;:;BRICK;:;BRICK;:;BRICK;:;BRI

;:;BRICK;:;BRICK;:;BRICK;:;BRICK;:;BRICK;:;BRICK;:;BRICK;:;BRICK;:;BRICK;:;

ICK;:;BRICK;:;BRICK;:;BRICK;:;BRICK;:;BRICK;:;BRICK;:;BRICK;:;BRICK;:;BRI

\\\new windows in deep steel boxes/// \\\new windows in deep steel boxes///

O (O)

O

#%*||| #%*||| #%*||| #%*||| #%*||| #%*||| #%*||| #%*|||

X

#%*||| #%*||| #%*||| #%*||| #%*||| #%*||| #%*||| #%*|||

O O (0)

\\\new windows in deep steel boxes/// \\\new windows in deep steel boxes///

;:;BRICK;:;BRICK;:;BRICK;:;BRICK;:;BRICK;:;BRICK;:;BRICK;:;BRICK;:;BRICK;:;

ICK;:;BRICK;:;BRICK;:;BRICK;:;BRICK;:;BRICK;:;BRICK;:;BRICK;:;BRICK;:;BRI

;:;BRICK;:;BRICK;:;BRICK;:;BRICK;:;BRICK;:;BRICK;:;BRICK;:;BRICK;:;BRICK;:;

\\\new windows in deep steel boxes/// \\\new windows in deep steel boxes///

The decks overlook and provide access to a shared single yard.

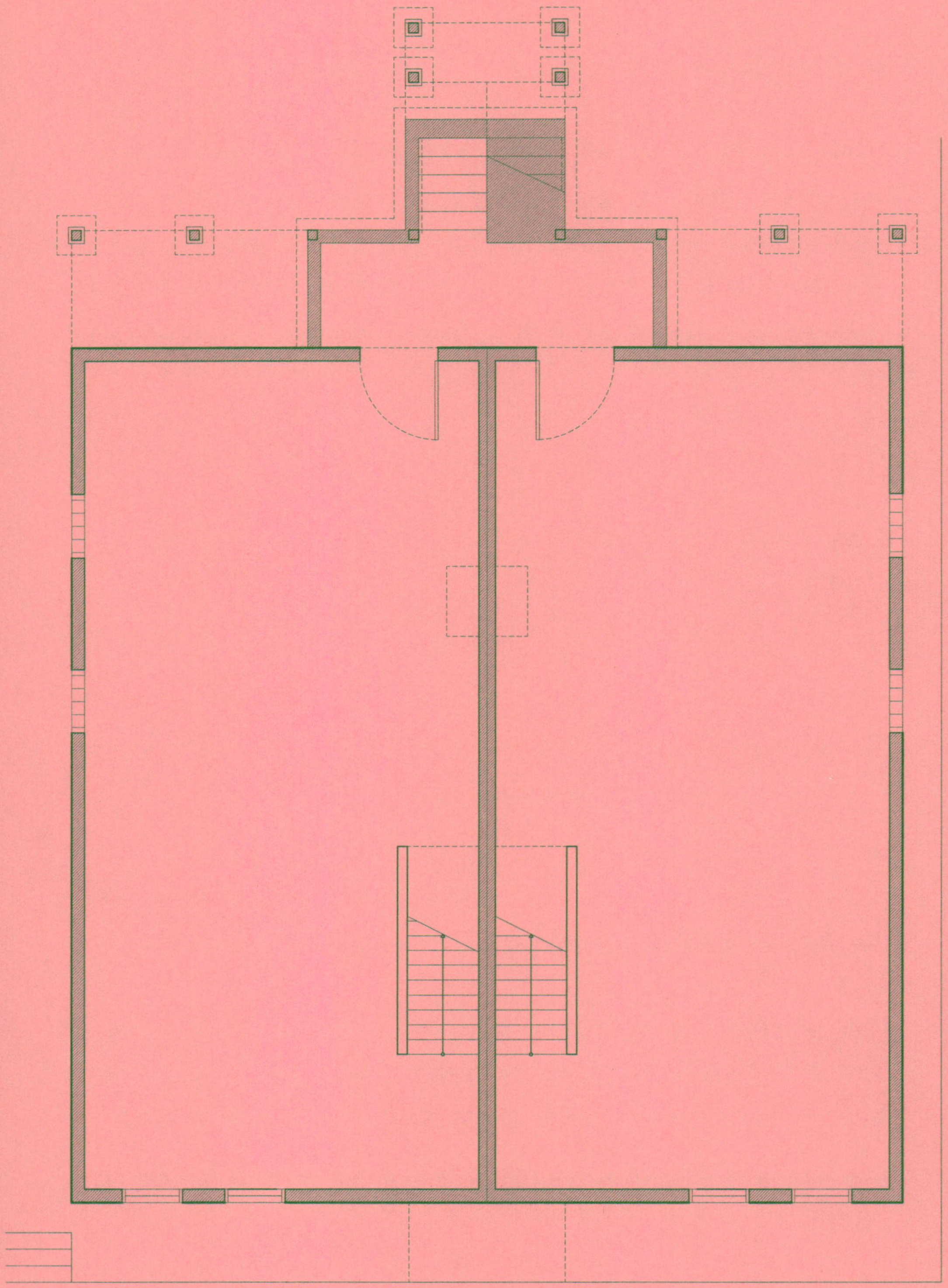

Plan (Basement)

Plan (Ground)

1824-22

Plan (Upper)

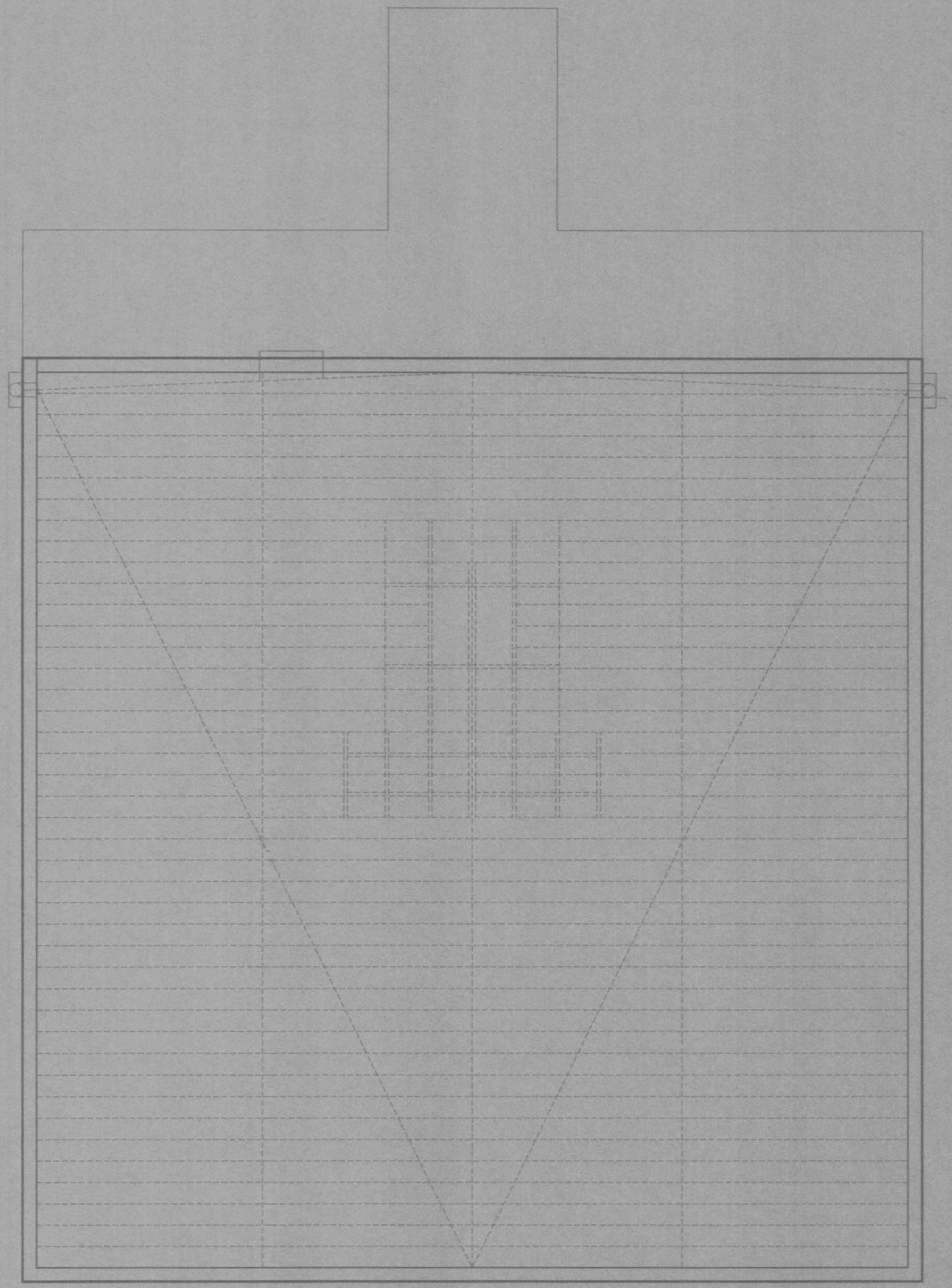

Plan (Roof)

1824-22

Photographs

^

// ..// ..// ..//   // ..// ..// ..//   // ..// ..// ..//   // ..// ..// ..//   // ../
/ ..// ..//
// ..// ..// ..//   // ..// ..// ..//   // ..// ..// ..//   // ..// ..// ..//   // ../
/ ..// ..//
// ..// ..// ..//   // ..// ..// ..//   // ..// ..// ..//   // ..// ..// ..//   // ../
/ ..// ..//
// ..// ..// ..//   // ..// ..// ..//   // ..// ..// ..//   // ..// ..// ..//   // ../
/ ..// ..//

A LOVE OFTHE WORLD

// ..// ..// ..//   // ..// ..// ..//   // ..// ..// ..//   // ..// ..// ..//   // ../
/ ..// ..//
// ..// ..// ..//   // ..// ..// ..//   // ..// ..// ..//   // ..// ..// ..//   // ../
/ ..// ..//

Qbert and Doctors Seuss and Spock: it is the building materials of old schools. It is a hallway cut thru chimneys staggered. And ultimately, it is not for you to decide what you like or not.

I mean sure, yeh of course, if everything's simple then everyone can be cool. But your situation isn't simple.

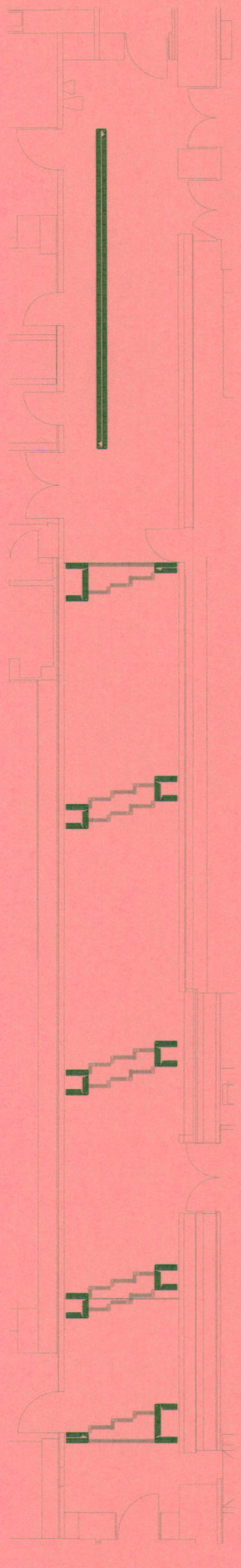

Plan (Gallery)

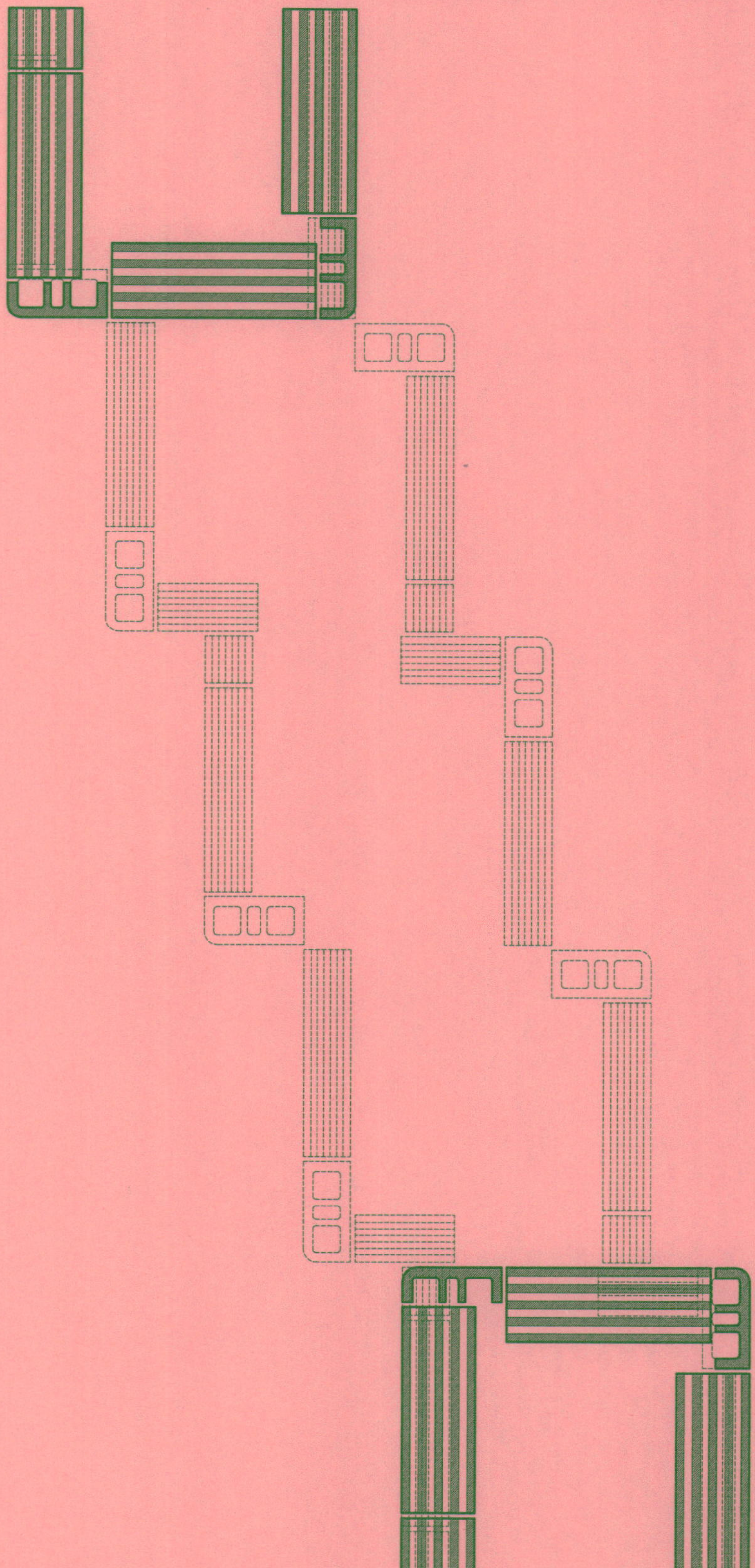

Plan (Detail)

Photographs

(a divorce) (a divorce) (a divorce)
(a divorce) (a divorce) (a divorce)
(a divorce) (a divorce) (a divorce)
(a divorce) (a divorce) (a divorce)
(a divorce) (a divorce) (a divorce)
(a divorce) (a divorce) (a divorce)
(a divorce) (a divorce) (a divorce)
(a divorce) (a divorce) (a divorce)
(a divorce) (a divorce) (a divorce)
(a divorce) (a divorce) (a divorce)
(a divorce) (a divorce) (a divorce)
(a divorce) (a divorce) (a divorce)
(a divorce) (a divorce) (a divorce)
(a divorce) (a divorce) (a divorce)
(a divorce) (a divorce) (a divorce)
(a divorce) (a divorce) (a divorce)
(a divorce) (a divorce) (a divorce)
(a divorce) (a divorce) (a divorce)
(a divorce) (a divorce) (a divorce)
(a divorce) (a divorce) (a divorce)
(a divorce) (a divorce) (a divorce)
(a divorce) (a divorce) (a divorce)
(a divorce) (a divorce) (a divorce)
(a divorce) (a divorce) (a divorce)
(a divorce) (a divorce) (a divorce)
(a divorce) (a divorce) (a divorce)
(a divorce) (a divorce) (a divorce)
(a divorce) (a divorce) (a divorce)
(a divorce) (a divorce) (a divorce)
(a divorce) (a divorce) (a divorce)
(a divorce) (a divorce) (a divorce)
(a divorce) (a divorce) (a divorce)
(a divorce) (a divorce) (a divorce)

(a divorce) (a divorce) (a divorce)
(a divorce) (a divorce) (a divorce)
(a divorce) (a divorce) (a divorce)
(a divorce) (a divorce) (a divorce)
(a divorce) (a divorce) (a divorce)
(a divorce) (a divorce) (a divorce)
(a divorce) (a divorce) (a divorce)
(a divorce) (a divorce) (a divorce)
(a divorce) (a divorce) (a divorce)
(a divorce) (a divorce) (a divorce)
(a divorce) (a divorce) (a divorce)
(a divorce) (a divorce) (a divorce)
(a divorce) (a divorce) (a divorce)
(a divorce) (a divorce) (a divorce)
(a divorce) (a divorce) (a divorce)
(a divorce) (a divorce) (a divorce)
(a divorce) (a divorce) (a divorce)
(a divorce) (a divorce) (a divorce)
(a divorce) (a divorce) (a divorce)
(a divorce) (a divorce) (a divorce)
(a divorce) (a divorce) (a divorce)
(a divorce) (a divorce) (a divorce)
(a divorce) (a divorce) (a divorce)
(a divorce) (a divorce) (a divorce)
(a divorce) (a divorce) (a divorce)
(a divorce) (a divorce) (a divorce)
(a divorce) (a divorce) (a divorce)
(a divorce) (a divorce) (a divorce)
(a divorce) (a divorce) (a divorce)
(a divorce) (a divorce) (a divorce)
(a divorce) (a divorce) (a divorce)
(a divorce) (a divorce) (a divorce)
(a divorce) (a divorce) (a divorce)

(a divorce) (a divorce) (a divorce)
(a divorce) (a divorce) (a divorce)
(a divorce) (a divorce) (a divorce)
(a divorce) (a divorce) (a divorce)
(a divorce) (a divorce) (a divorce)
(a divorce) (a divorce) (a divorce)
(a divorce) (a divorce) (a divorce)
(a divorce) (a divorce) (a divorce)
(a divorce) (a divorce) (a divorce)
(a divorce) (a divorce) (a divorce)
(a divorce) (a divorce) (a divorce)
(a divorce) (a divorce) (a divorce)
(a divorce) (a divorce) (a divorce)
(a divorce) (a divorce) (a divorce)
(a divorce) (a divorce) (a divorce)
(a divorce) (a divorce) (a divorce)
(a divorce) (a divorce) (a divorce)
(a divorce) (a divorce) (a divorce)
(a divorce) (a divorce) (a divorce)
(a divorce) (a divorce) (a divorce)
(a divorce) (a divorce) (a divorce)
(a divorce) (a divorce) (a divorce)
(a divorce) (a divorce) (a divorce)
(a divorce) (a divorce) (a divorce)
(a divorce) (a divorce) (a divorce)
(a divorce) (a divorce) (a divorce)
(a divorce) (a divorce) (a divorce)
(a divorce) (a divorce) (a divorce)
(a divorce) (a divorce) (a divorce)
(a divorce) (a divorce) (a divorce)
(a divorce) (a divorce) (a divorce)
(a divorce) (a divorce) (a divorce)
(a divorce) (a divorce) (a divorce)

A VISIT

There must be geometric rules dating back thousands of years that The Greeks articulated and we'd all recognize as indisputable when we come across them exemplified in the world. And when we see these rules demonstrated and contradicted even just a smidge, it feels even more right. That's how it is, everything.

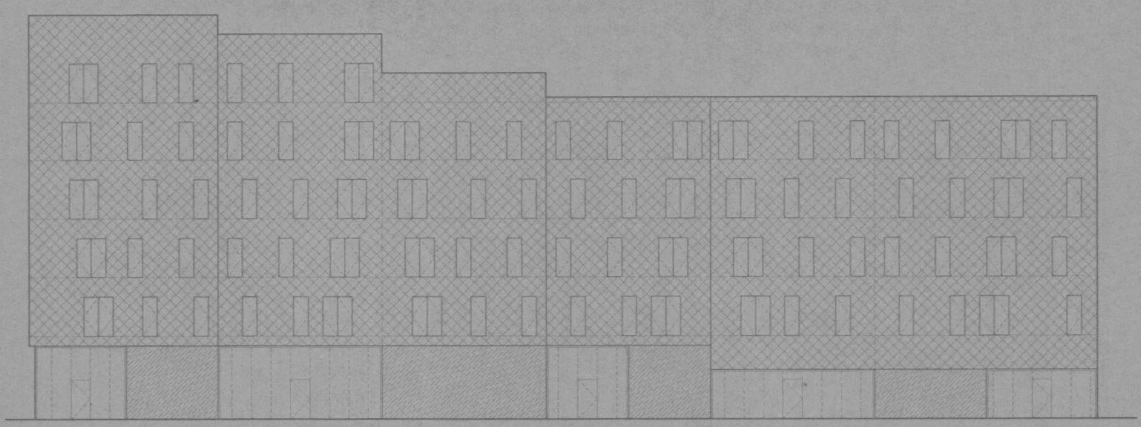

Elevation (West)

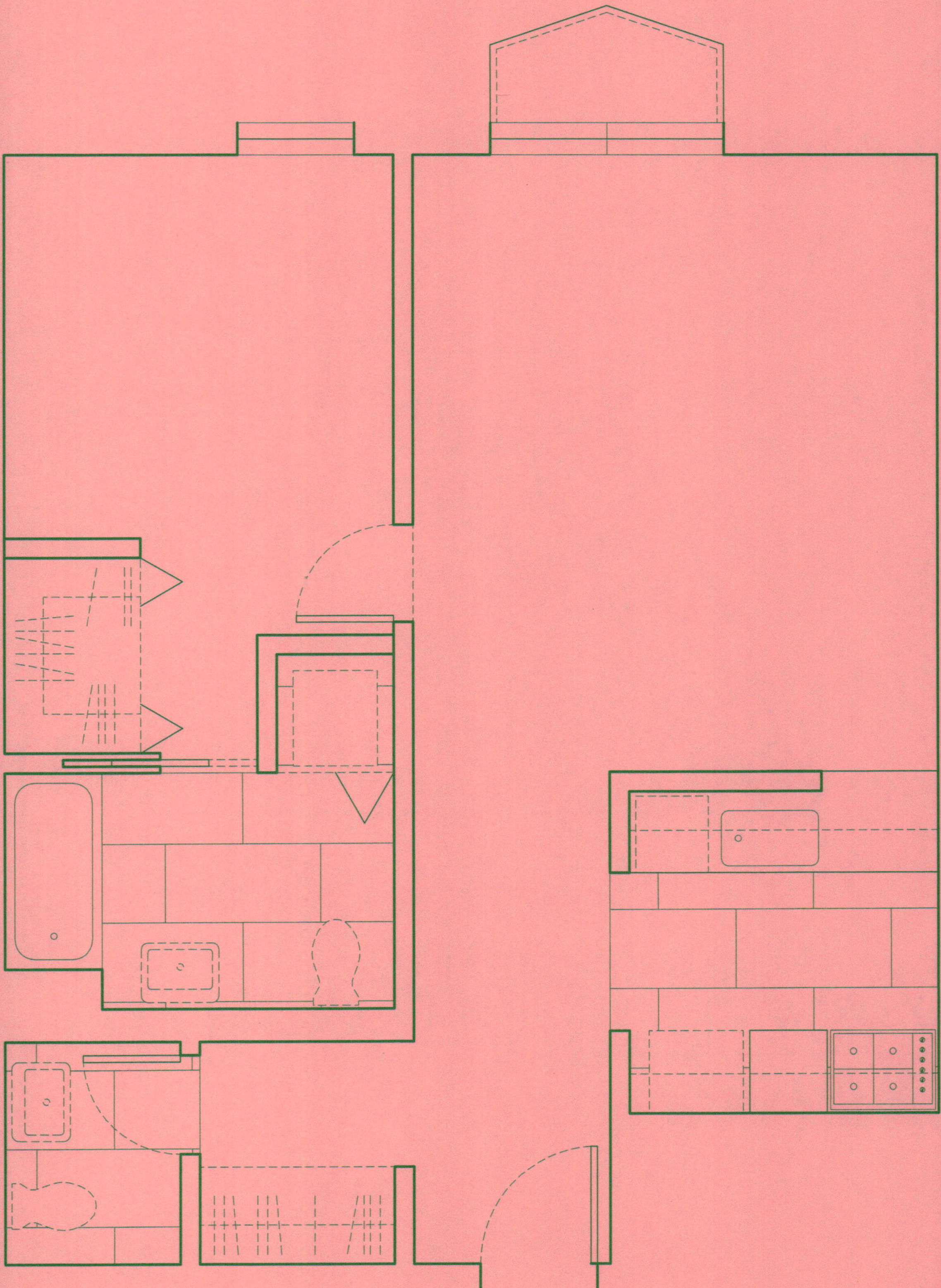

Plan (Typical 1-bedroom)

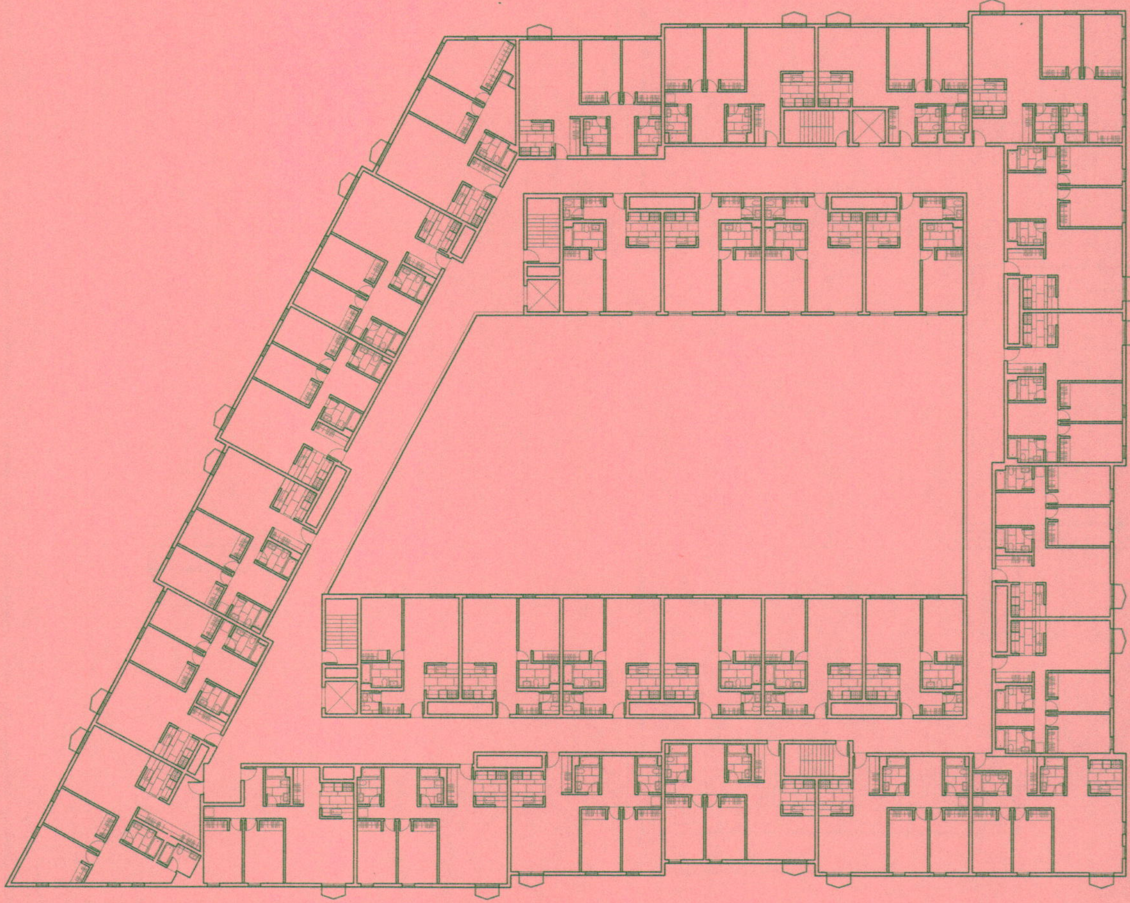

Plan (Typical)

173RD STREET
173RD STREET
67TH AVENUE
OAK PARK AVENUE
NORTH STREET
NORTH

Site Plan

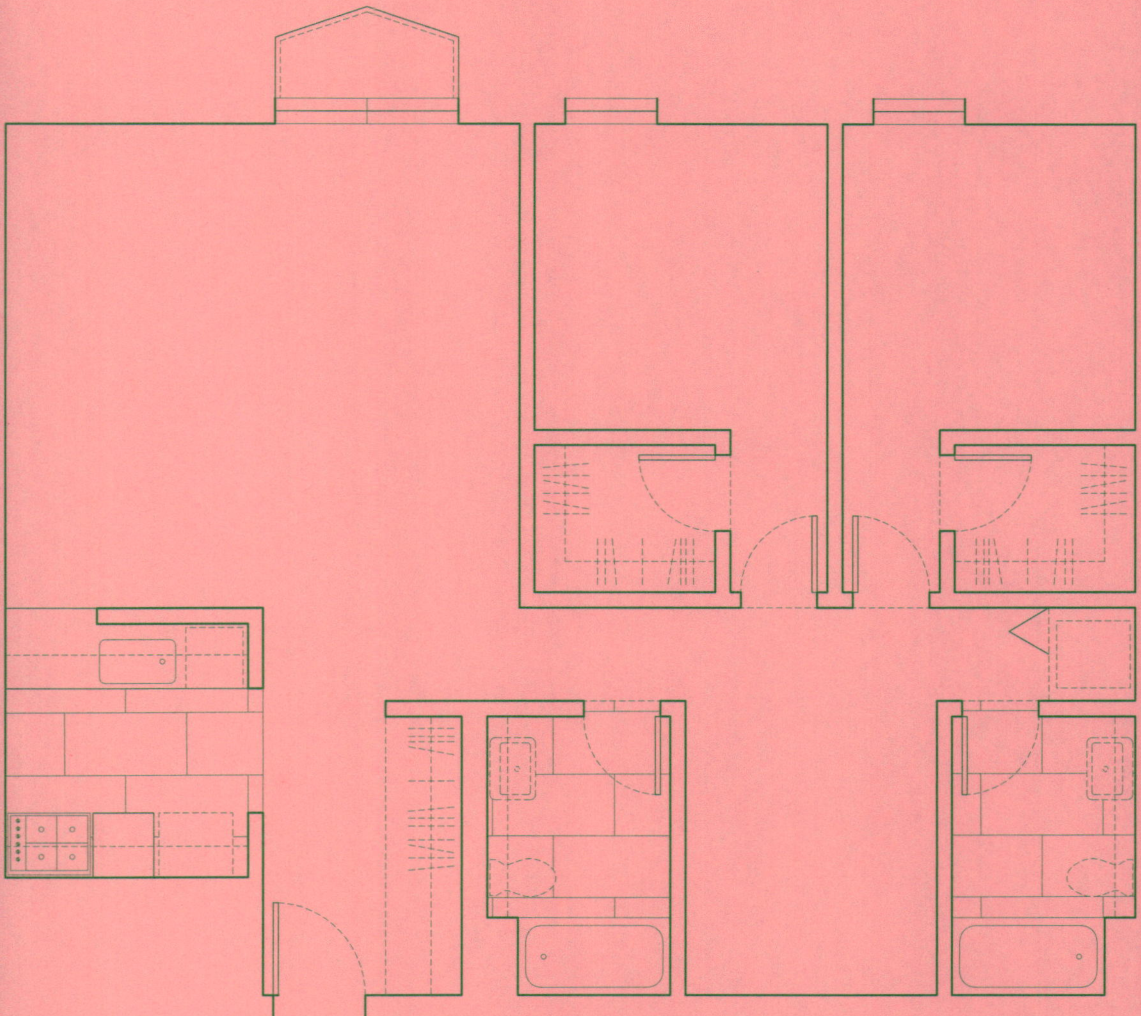

Plan (Typical 2-bedroom)

H1 p.220

```
                                      ^
                                     / \
                                    /   \
                                   /     \
                                  /       \
                                 /         \
                                /           \
                               /             \
                              /
_____________                /
|     |     |               /                          R
| ART | ART |                                        E
|_____|_____|                                      V
|     |                                          I
| ART |                                        R
|_____|                                      E
                                           V
exposed local stones embedded in the build I
                                 R
                                    E
                                  V
                                I
                              R
```

When you cut skylights the same shape and size as boxes strewn about the room, when the walls are repetitive and dense, but sans pattern, and the angles of everything are all staged entropy, yes a moment freezes, a collapsing suspended, a verb and its tension, potential stressed—That, in buildings, as buildings.

Robert Anton Wilson has this thing about the history of power and how churches always used to be the tallest building in town, and then later it was the government buildings, and now it's corporations.

It'd be cool to make little models of that out of the pages of The Communist Manifesto.

And then you can show it to everyone in one of these short art buildings.

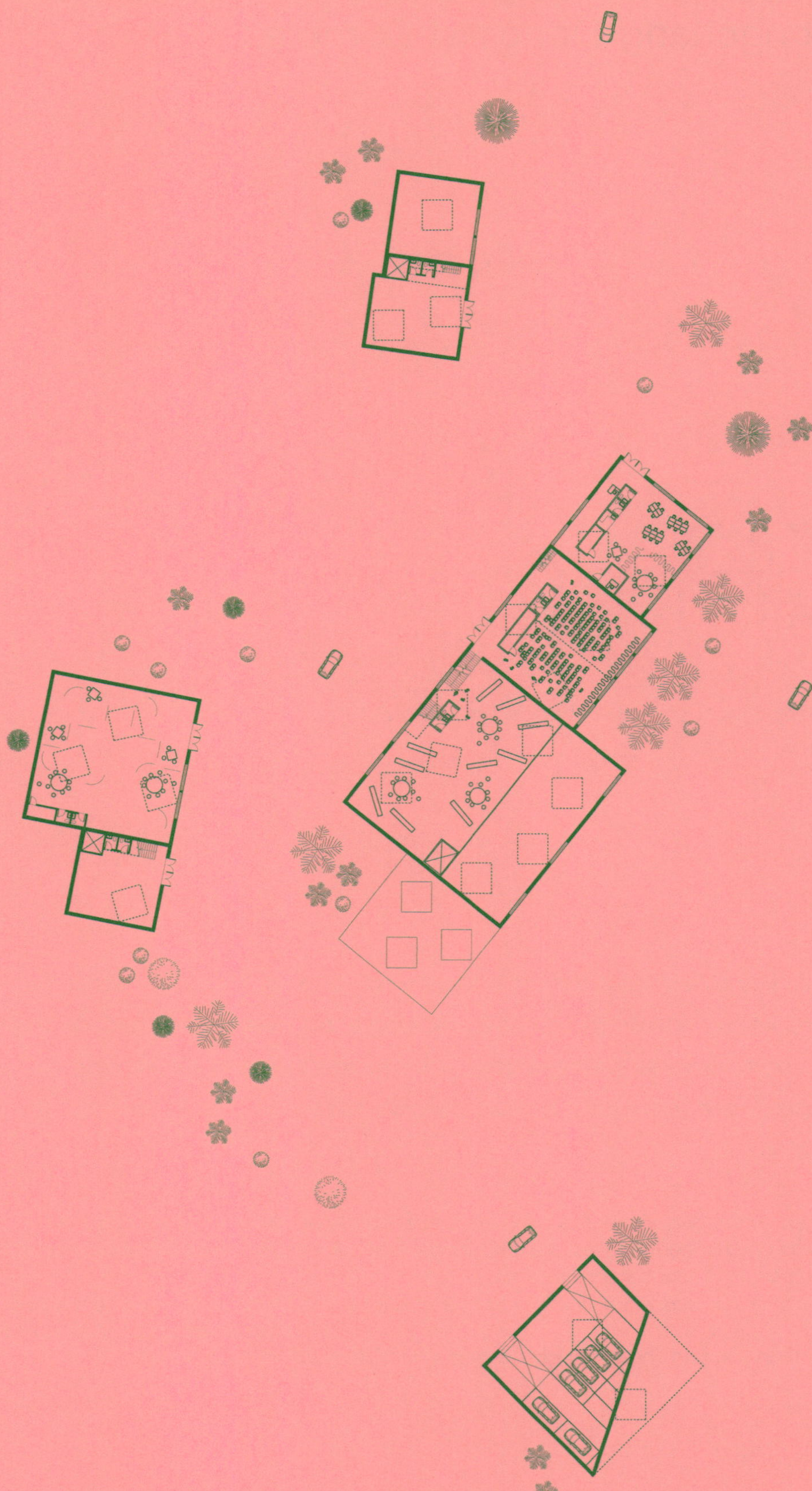

Site Plan

Section (Gallery)

Photographs

nu

There are no windows on the exterior, but there are windows on the interior.

How all the gray and fuzz makes dim rainbow light pop, just at the seams, but an ouroboros, folded across its bends, and the simplest baffles standing jut. Yes it is new and yes undoing is part of what it does.

It's been cool getting to see each other like this, getting to know each other again.

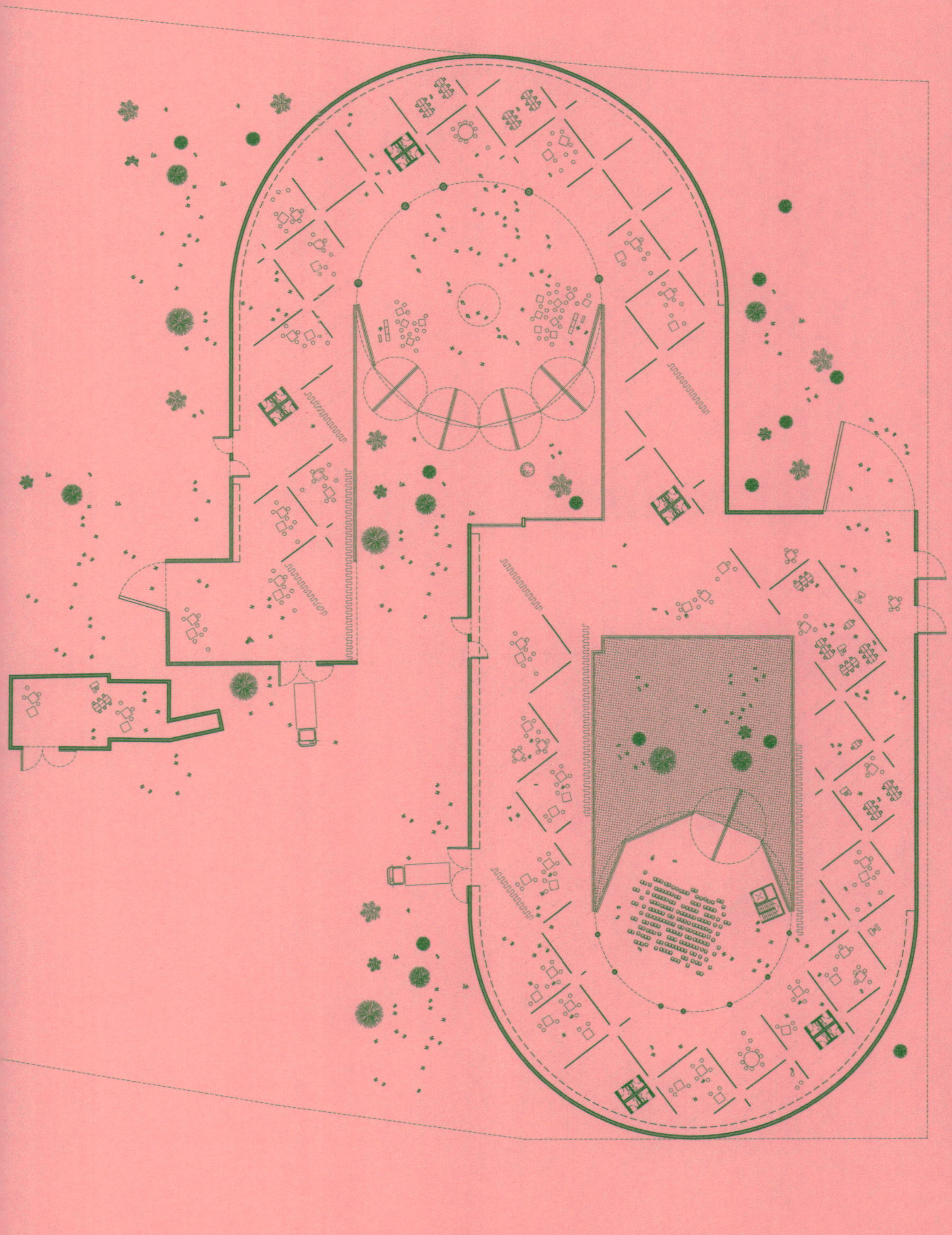

Plan (Ground)

Photographs

J1 p.42
J2 p.54
J3 p.237

THE LAKE

~`~`~`~`~`~`~`~`~`~`~`~`~`~`~`~`~`~`~`~`~`~`~`~`~`~`~`~`~`~`~

~`~`~`~`~`~`~`~`~`~`~`~`~`~`~`~`~`~`~`~`~`~`~`~`~`~`~`~`~`~`~

——————————————————————————————————

00.000.00&` ^v^V^v^ **+#\ +#\ (^(~~~** `% 000.00000.
00

000.000.000..0`%—— —~~ +#\ +#** ^v^V^v^
&`000.000.0

00&` ^v^V^v^**+#\00——.,.,.,(^(~~~**——<><><00.000.00.00\\000.0

00.000.000`% **(.,(~~~ ——————^v^V^v^ details_000.000.00.0

00.0\\000.normal^V^v^**+#\..—(^(~~~** `%000.000) \ ///000.000

XXXXXXXXXXXXXXXXXXXXXXXXXXXXXXXXXXXXXXXXXXXXXXXX

XXXXXXXXXXXXXXXXXXXXXXXXXXXXXXXXXXXXXXXXXXXXXXXX

XXXXXXXXXXXXXXXXXXXXXXXXXXXXXXXXXXXXXXXXXXXXXXXX

XXXXXXXXXXXXXXXXXXXXXXXXXXXXXXXXXXXXXXXXXXXXXXXX

XXXXXXXXXXXXXXXXXXXXXXXXXXXXXXXXXXXXXXXXXXXXXXXX

We all always live in grayscales of green, and beige set aside white, obstructing or allowing light, how it piles on itself and becomes one thing. All that is common. It's normal.

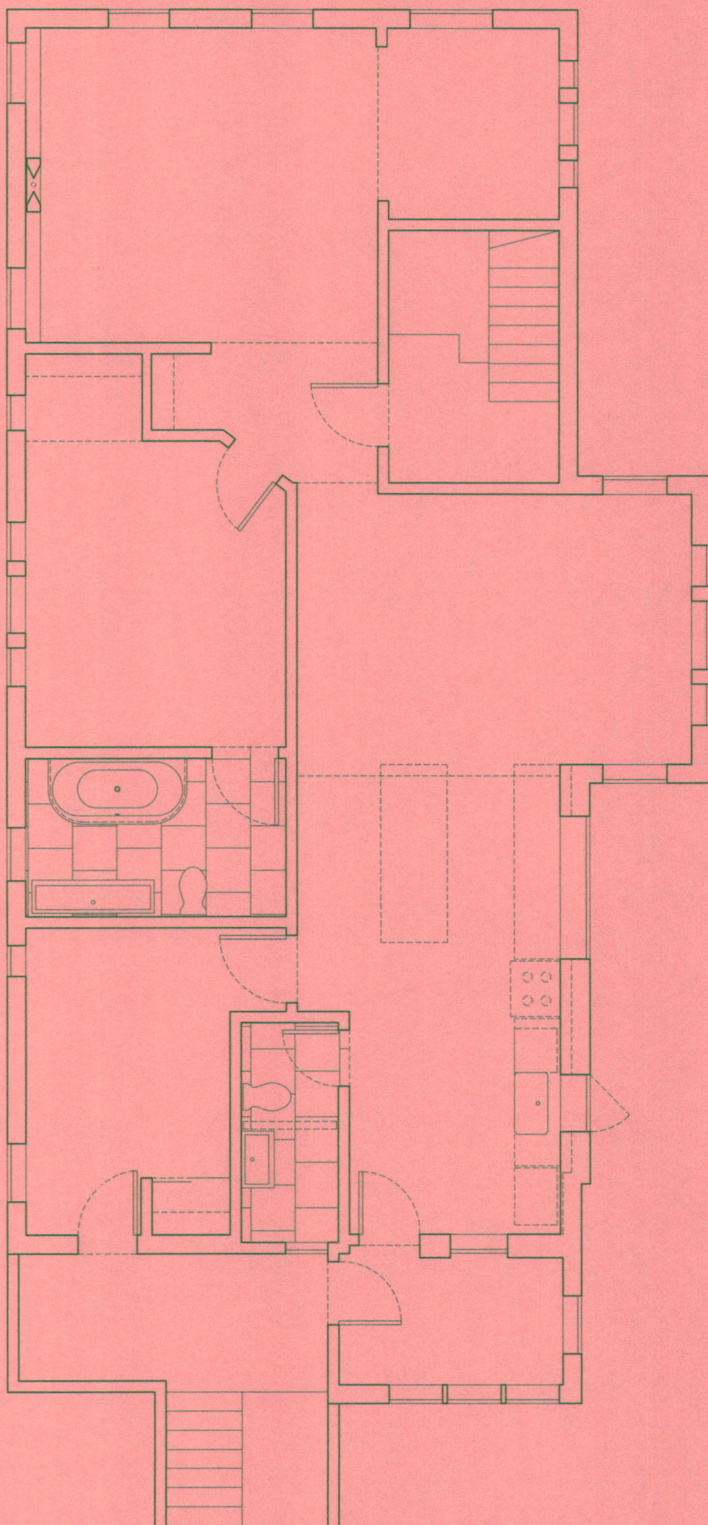

Plan

Apartment 2

Photographs

THE LAKE

~`~`~`~`~`~`~`~`~`~`~`~`~`~`~`~`~`~`~`~`~`~`~`~`~`~`~`~`~`~`~`~`~`~`~`~`~`~`~`~
~`~`~`~`~`~`~`~`~`~`~`~`~`~`~`~`~`~`~`~`~`~`~`~`~`~`~`~`~`~`~`~`~`~`~`~`~`~`~`~

the bean

Mmm num ba de

{*}

Dum bum ba be

Doo buh dum ba beh beh
Pressure pushing down on me
Pressing down on you, no man ask for

```
                    __________
     /\           \##########/
    /::::::::::::\    \######/
   /:::::::::::::::::::\       \/
```

people on streets
Um ba ba be
Um ba ba be
De day da
Ee day da, that's okay
It's the terror of knowing what the world is about
Watching some good friends scream
"Let me out!"

Ee do ba be
Ee da ba ba ba
Um bo bo
Be lap
People on streets
Ee da de da de
People on streets
Ee da de da de da de da

Can't we give ourselves one more chance?

Gates at angles and bath blue, you can be inside and outside simultaneously— strange intersections create different depths depending on your perspective. How to set up a metal tent in public so that if it's somehow not weird, that means everything's weird. Like trees, every tree common and completely unique.

Isometric Drawing

Kind of Boring

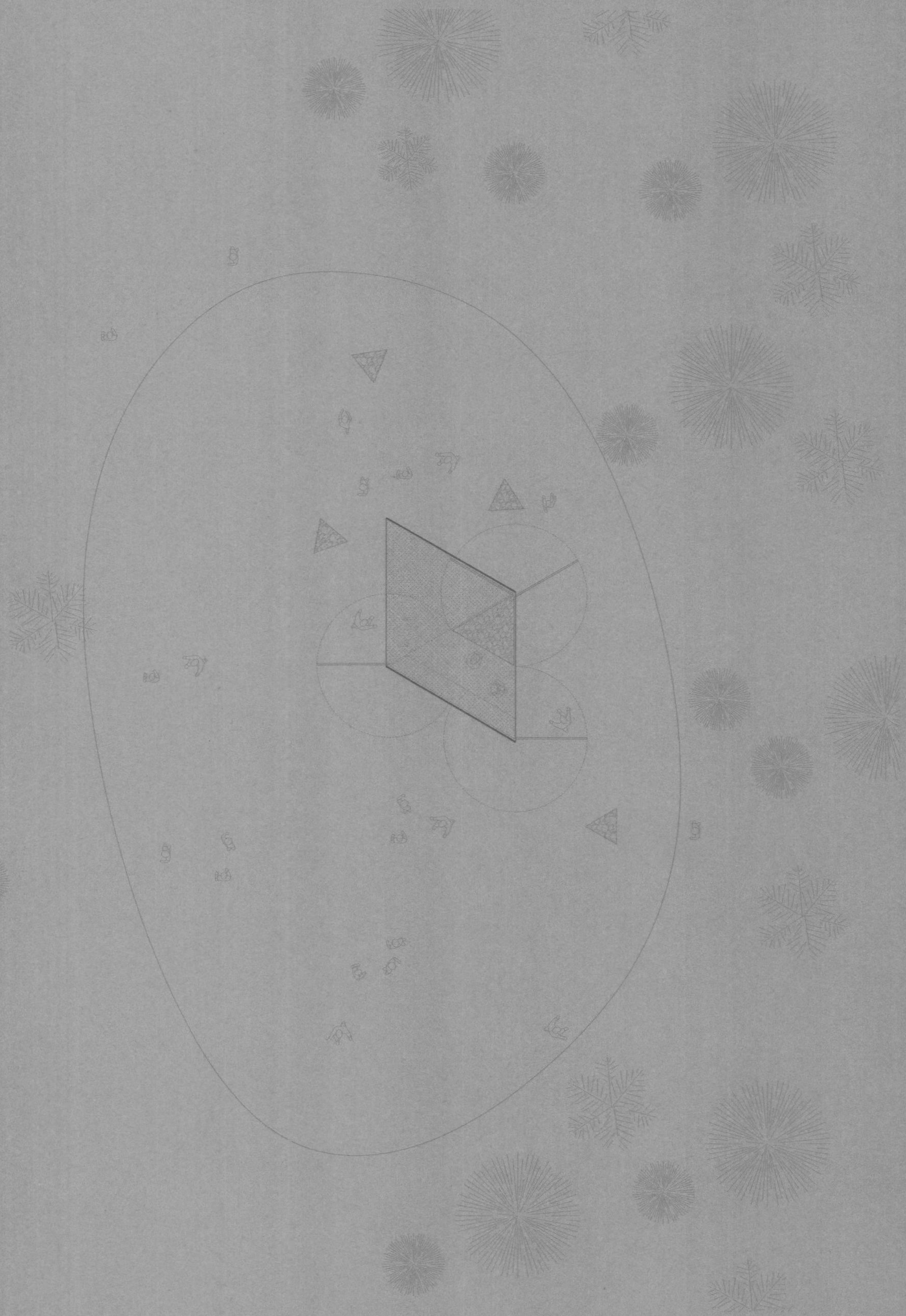

Site Plan

Photographs

```
     /\
    / \
   /    \
  /      \    /\
 /        \ /   \       !
/          \/         \     !
            \     \     !              !
                        !              !
                        !              !
                        ! /\                !
                        !/   \             !
                        !    \             /\
                        /\      \
        [::::::::::]   /||\         \
```

[::::::::::] also a little bit annoying when simply trying to walk to the other side

```
Just imagine the effect when something so simple that
we commonly fail to even recognize it as a tool, gets
its scale warped and context tweaked. Set up the dining
room set on the lawn, park the lawnmower in the living
room.
```

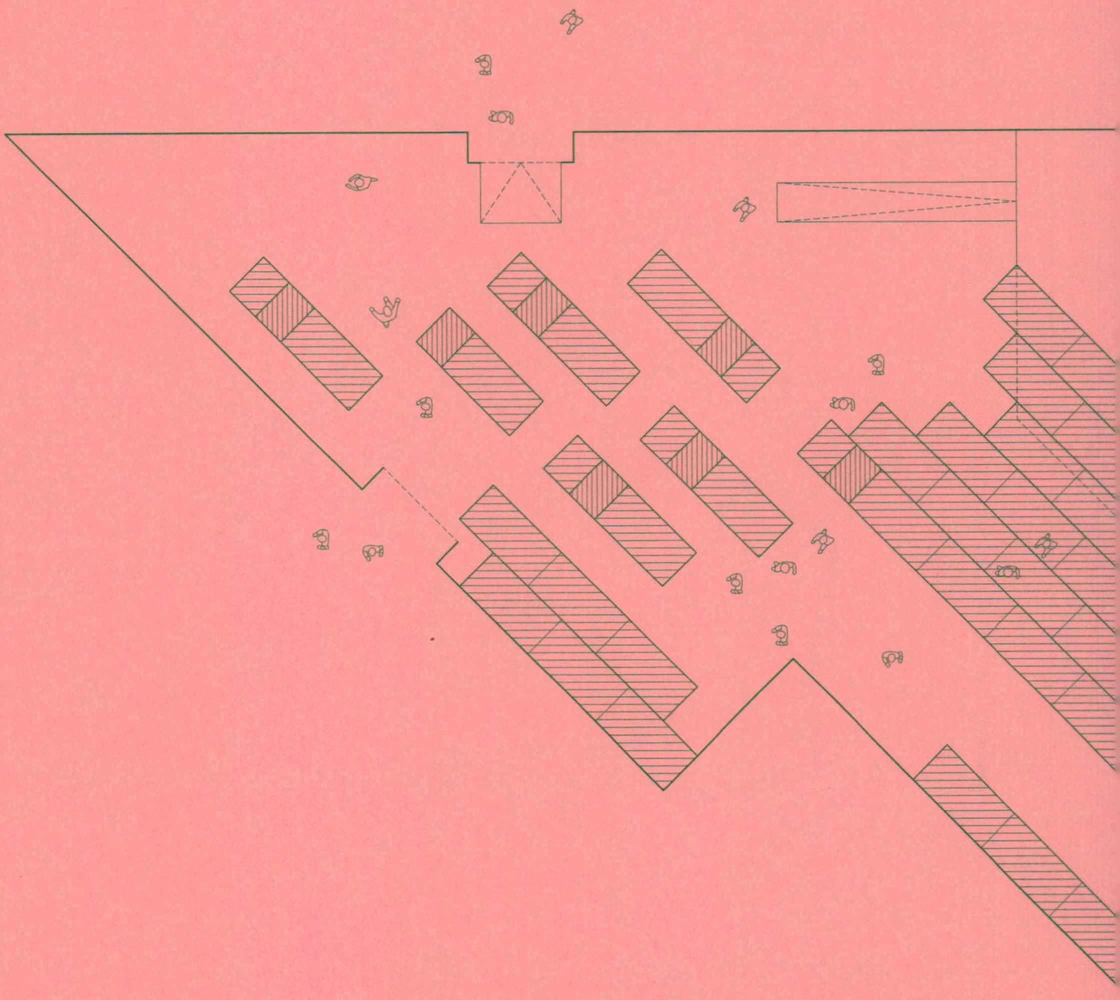

Plan

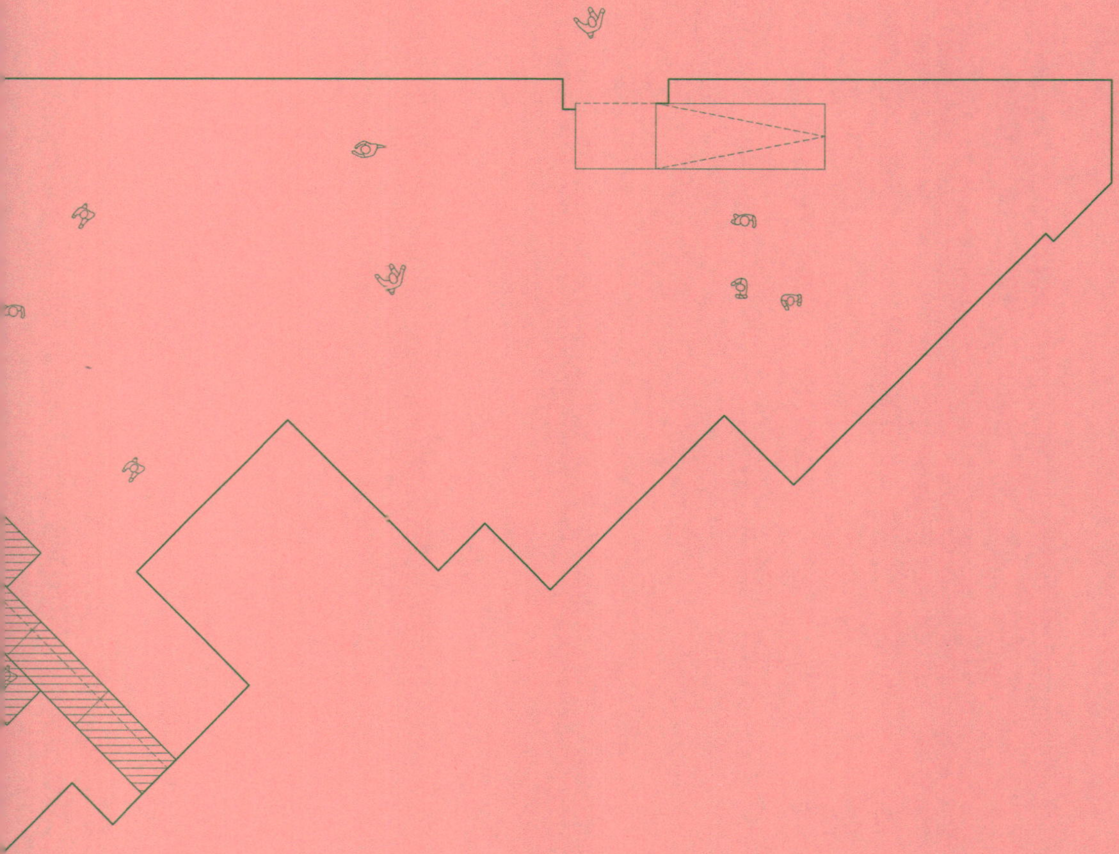

Photographs

(
(
(
(
(
(
(
(
(((
(((((
(((((((
(((((((((
(((((((((((
((((((((((((((
(((((((((((((((((

(((((ART~~COMMUNITY~~SELF~~past~~future~~present

Open so that the inside can appear to unfold outwards, but maintaining its shape. Its facade—the interruption of flat, bold blocks across swimming stones—a model reenacting how the buildings sit in the valley, in the present.

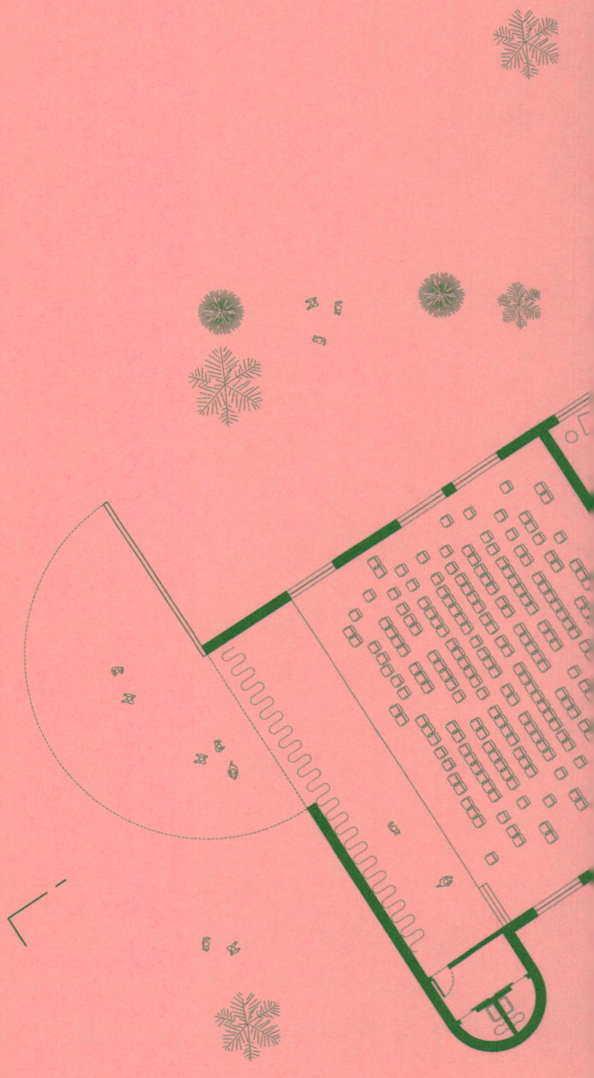

Plan (Ground)

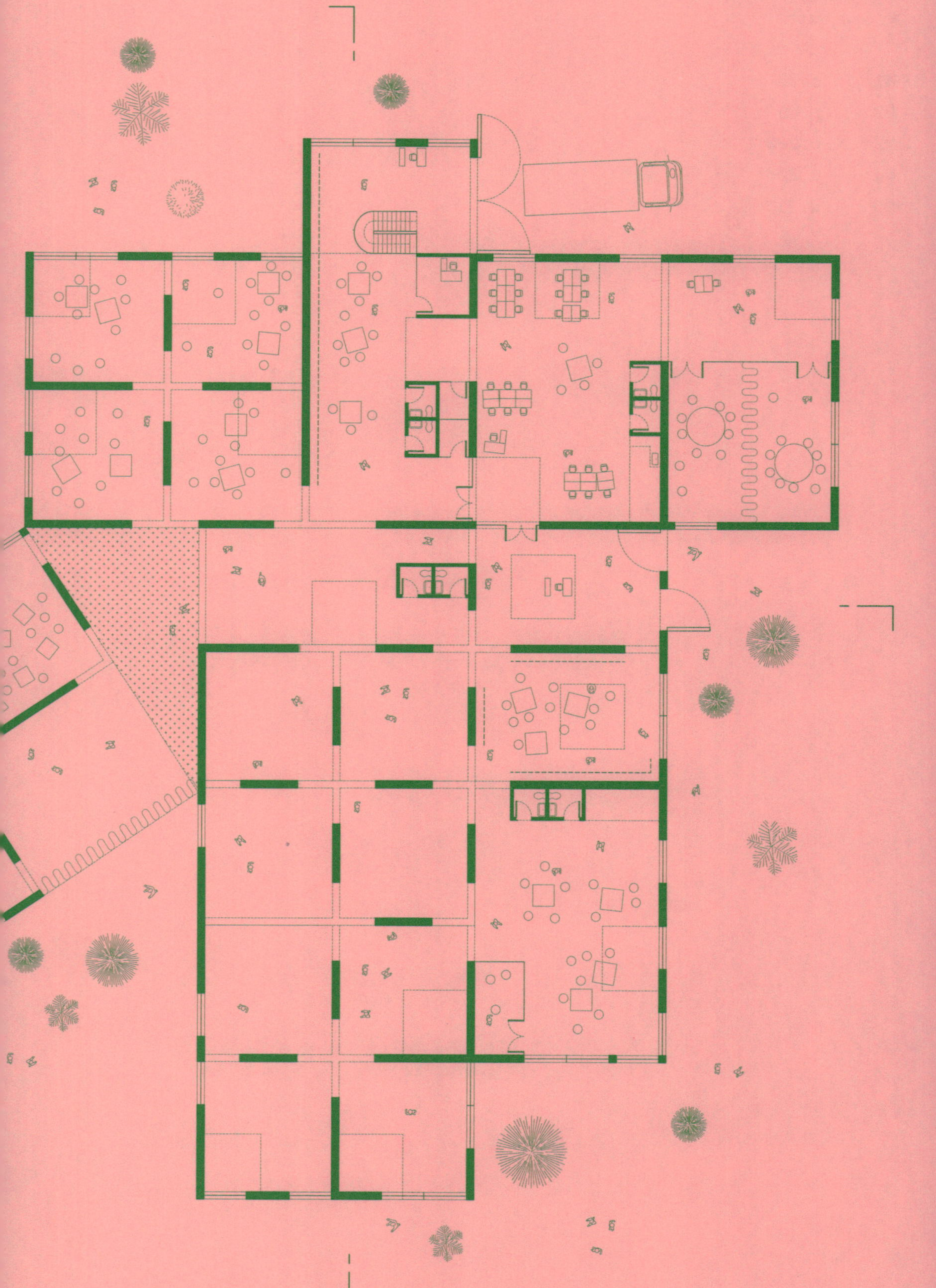

Photographs

2B2B2B2B2B2B2B2B2B2B2B2B2B2B2B2B2B2B2B2B2B2B2B2B2B2B2B2B2B2B2B2B

B4 B4 B4 B4 B4 B4 B4 B4 B4 B4 B4 B4 B4 B4 B4 B4 B4 B4 B4 B4 B4 B4 B4 B4

111111111111111111111111111111 AAAAAAAAAAAAAAAAAAAA
111111111111111111111111111111 AAAAAAAAAAAAAAAAAAAA
111111111111111111111111111111 AAAAAAAAAAAAAAAAAAAA
111111111111111111111111111111 AAAAAAAAAAAAAAAAAAAA
111111111111111111111111111111 AAAAAAAAAAAAAAAAAAAA
111111111111111111111111111111 AAAAAAAAAAAAAAAAAAAA
111111111111111111111111111111 AAAAAAAAAAAAAAAAAAAA
111111111111111111111111111111 AAAAAAAAAAAAAAAAAAAA
111111111111111111111111111111 AAAAAAAAAAAAAAAAAAAA
111111111111111111111111111111 AAAAAAAAAAAAAAAAAAAA
111111111111111111111111111111 AAAAAAAAAAAAAAAAAAAA
111111111111111111111111111111 AAAAAAAAAAAAAAAAAAAA
111111111111111111111111111111 AAAAAAAAAAAAAAAAAAAA
111111111111111111111111111111 AAAAAAAAAAAAAAAAAAAA
111111111111111111111111111111 AAAAAAAAAAAAAAAAAAAA
111111111111111111111111111111 AAAAAAAAAAAAAAAAAAAA
111111111111111111111111111111 AAAAAAAAAAAAAAAAAAAA
111111111111111111111111111111 AAAAAAAAAAAAAAAAAAAA

B4 B4 B4 B4 B4 B4 B4 B4 B4 B4 B4 B4 B4 B4 B4 B4 B4 B4 B4 B4 B4 B4 B4 B4

To live within an exploded beige and white yin yang, organized according to stacked cabinets, surrounded by skyline from up inside it, to be absorbed into non-dualistic systems

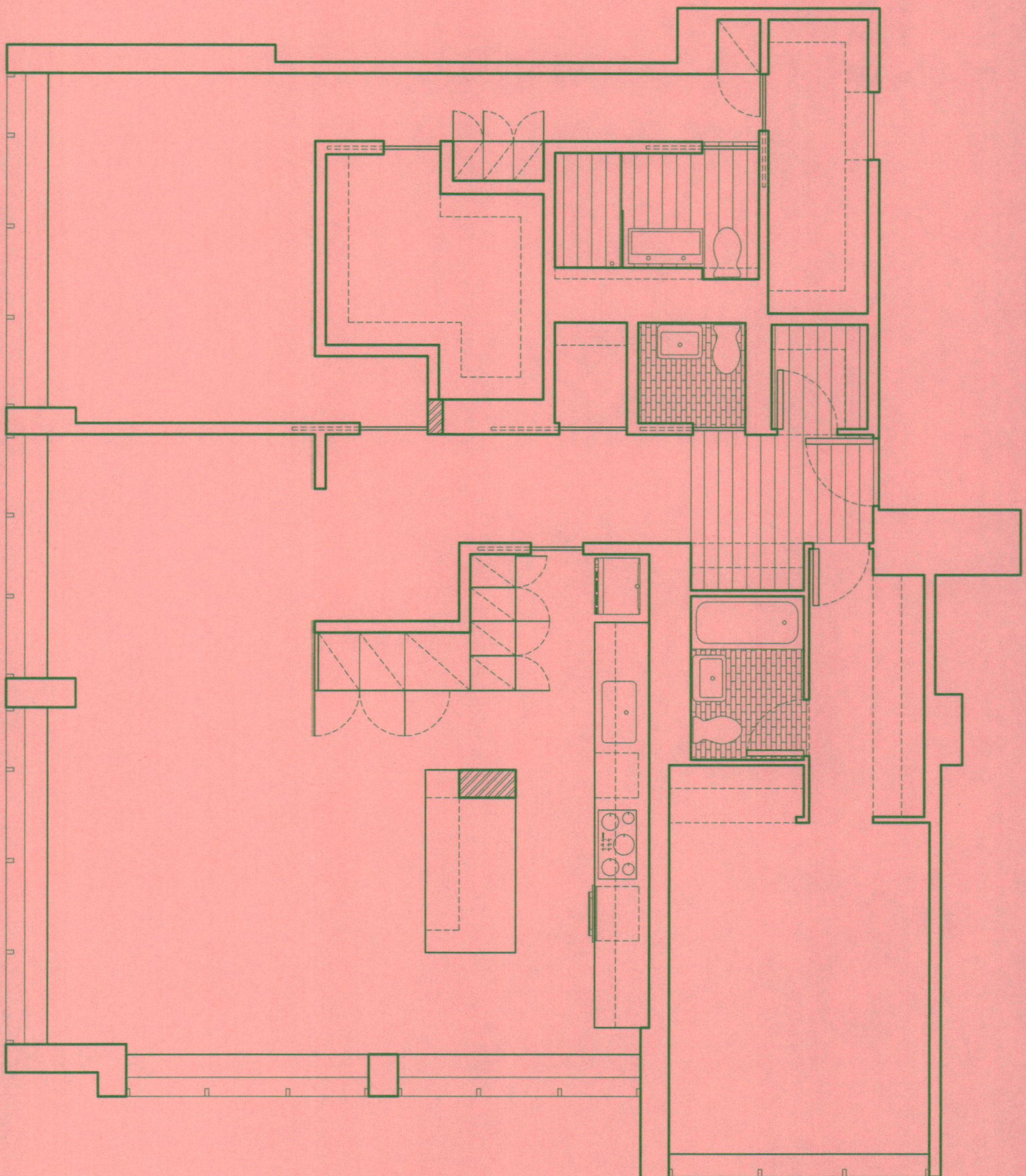

Plan

Apartment 1A

Photographs

```
                                                _____________________________
                                                |                                   |
                                                |          oversized                |
                                      ________|_______________plain_______ |
~`~`                                  a composition of ..................  |      |
~`~`                                  shapes proposes a democracy of       |      |
~`~`                                  functions within.                    |      |
 ~`~`                                 |                                    |____ |
  ~`~`                                |                                    |
   ~`~`                               |____________ WELCOME_______ |
     ~`~`                                 / /
       ~`~`                              / /
          ~`~`                          / /
              ~`~`                     / /
                  ~`~`               / /
                    ~`~` ~`~`/ /
                                   /~`~`~`~`~`~`~`~`~`~`~`~`~`~`~`~`~`~`~`~`~`~`~`~`~`
                                        ~`~`~`~`~`~`~`~`~`~`~`~`~`~`~`~`~`~`~`~`~`~`~`
```

How are we expected to scale our imaginations? What shock comes from the simplest twists and pivots? How colors depend on each other, muted and otherwise. How big folds can be. How balance is hitting the right ratio of the appearance of disorganization. Two lives of everything: day and night.

Big things, dumb things, boring things: they're all like self-aware intentional gestures, him being generous to whoever uses the space, being generous to their way of using it.

Plan (Ground)

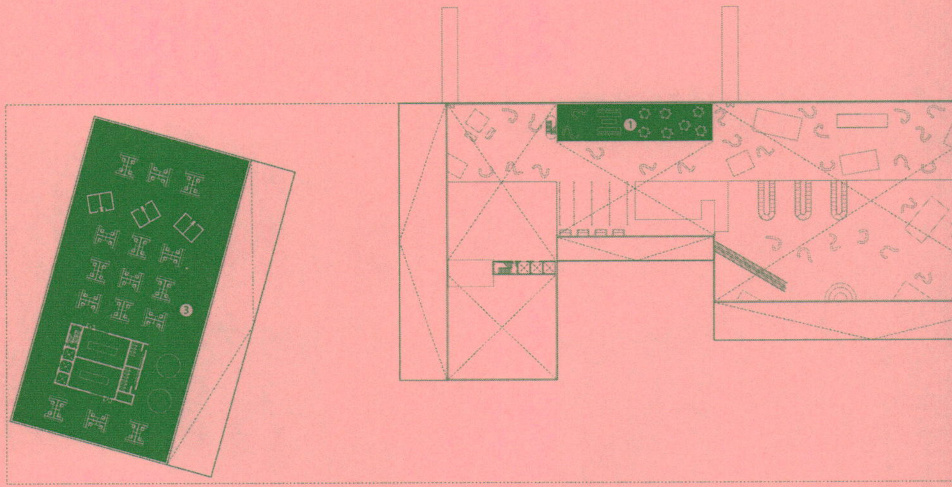

Plan (15m)

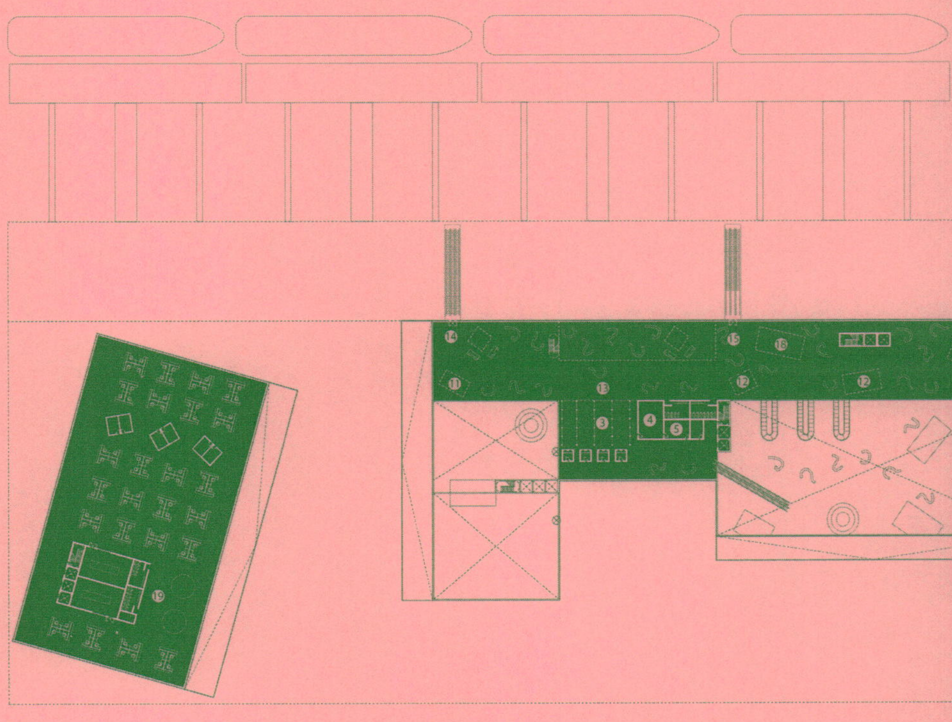

Plan (10m)

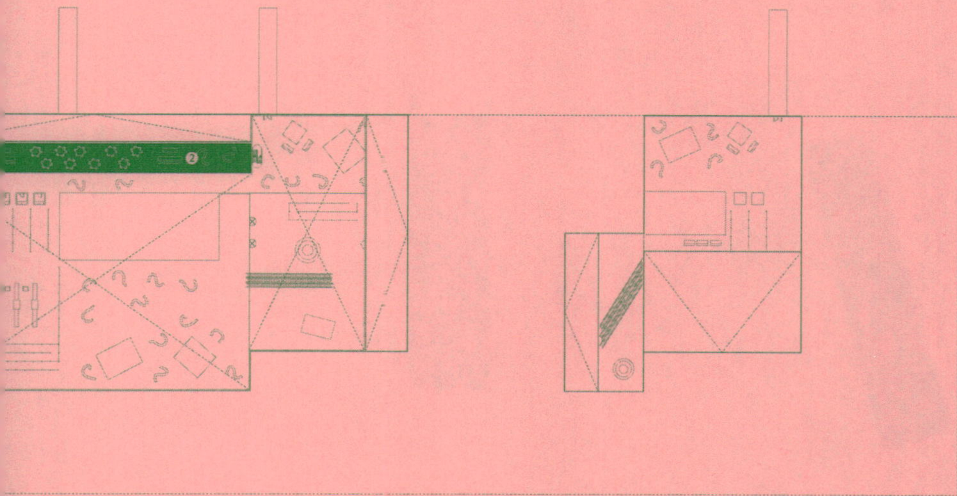

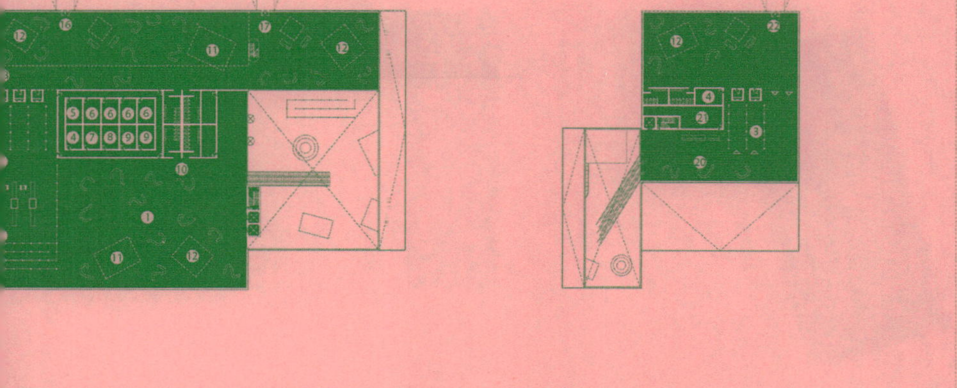

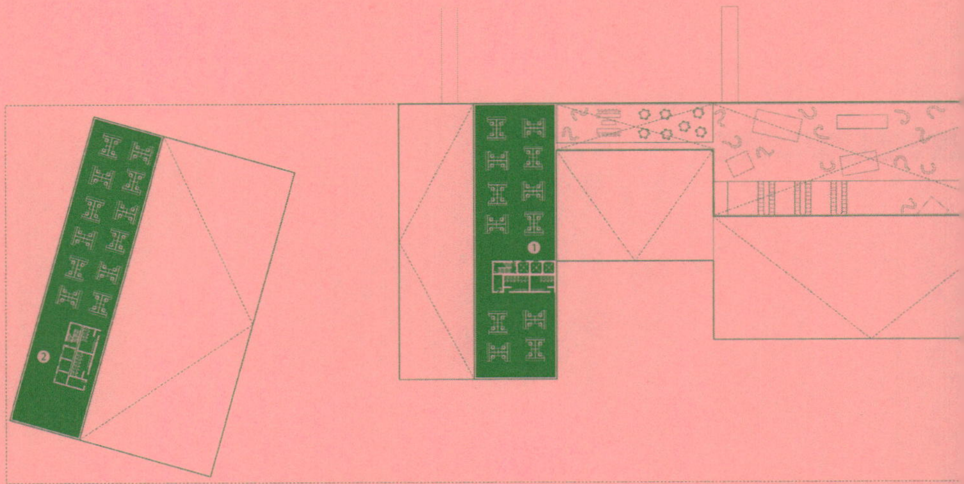

Plan (Typ)

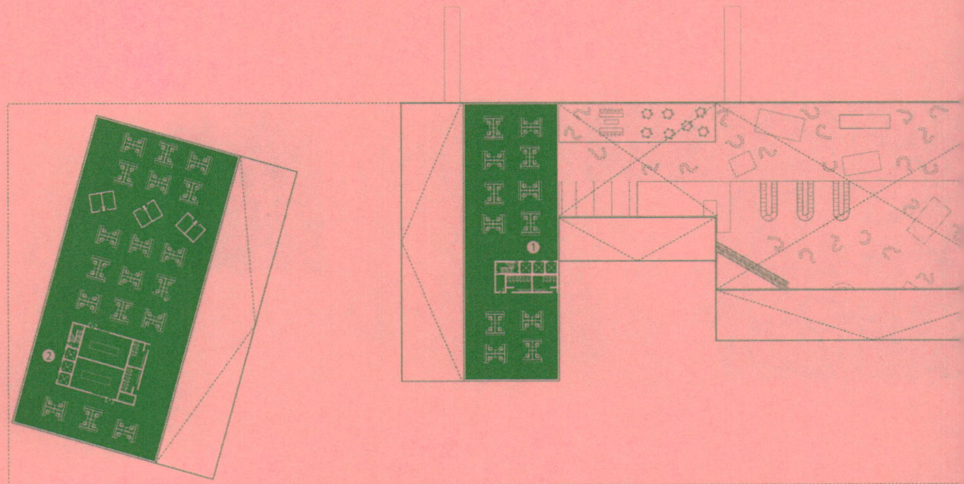

Plan (20m)

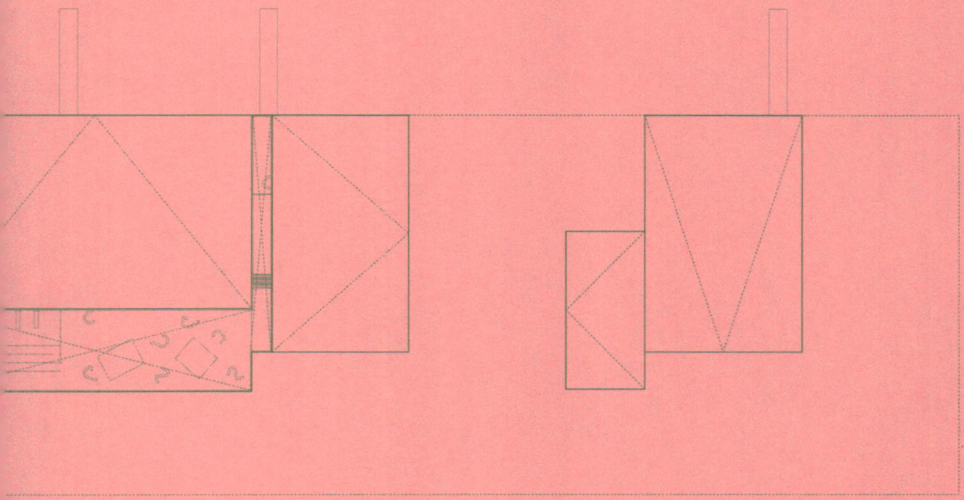

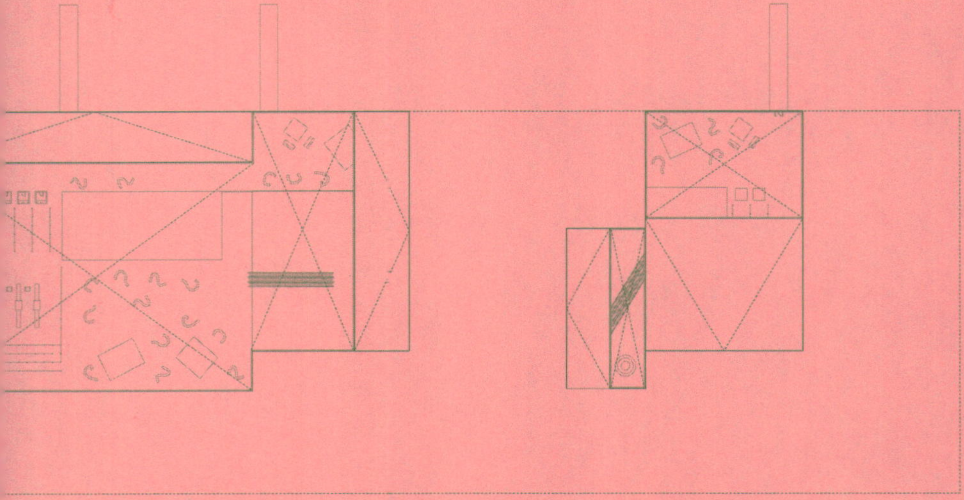

Photographs

American Textures

Jayne Kelley

My Favorite Shapes is a 2019 HBO special featuring the Salvadoran comedy writer Julio Torres. It is organized such that for the better part of an hour, Torres sits behind a thin conveyor belt that he operates with a pedal, which conveys to him a series of small objects—the "shapes" of the title. Certain shapes are pretenses for story-jokes, some personal, some invented. Other shapes get only the slightest explanation. Torres is wearing a shiny silver r obe and matching pants; his shoes are clear plastic with white soles; his shaggy hair is platinum blond, with dark roots; he has dabbed silver glitter from his cheekbones to his temples. He occasionally complains about the order in which the shapes are arriving, as if there's been a bureaucratic mix-up backstage.

Torres's shapes are not shapes—they are objects, even when they are simple ones. And they also aren't really his, even if his comedy is idiosyncratic. His work is to lift the contours of the thing from the thing itself so we can find something more there, inside and around it.

Near the end of the hour, he digresses from a joke to make a pointed remark, one of several in the special. "My least favorite shape is someone telling me 'It is what it is,'" he says. Cut to me, floored. I might have teared up, but I also get emotional pretty easily.

I've had this idea of "American textures" in my mind relative to Paul's work since he asked me to write for this book, long before I saw *My Favorite Shapes*. I was thinking particularly of *Five Rooms*, the installation he completed with Paul Andersen for the 2017 Chicago Architecture Biennial. What struck me more than the strange profiles of these tiled archways was the framing they suddenly provided, not of the photographs on the walls—though that too—but of the water fountain and wall clock at the end of the forlorn public corridor. This framing is less literal than material. The tile is shiny but so municipal; I felt I was in a public school. Similar is the expanded steel sheet that splits the elegant arch of Summer Vault: it's a matte electric sky blue, like the installation as a whole but also so municipal; the vault feels like a playground. These parts of projects are too willingly reliant on material qualities to become image, though they get close. I started to think of them as textures.

Armed with this hammer, I found plenty of nails: the blown-up terrazzo ground in the City-County Building Plaza; the scaleless yet visceral white foam of *Foam Thing*; the perforations of DAR Al Uloum Library; the "featureless" white cement siding and "anti-material" oak boards on the facade of the Morris House. This textural quality is especially present in the colorful, corrugated concrete of the Ring of Hope sports center. In a write-up of the project after its P/A Award, architecture critic Blair Kamin explains ("needless to say") that padding should be installed to prevent athletes from hurting themselves when they inevitably run into the walls. The texture of this building is so compelling that it makes some of us forget that regular walls are pretty hard, too.

The term "texture" has an ambiguous history within architecture. I think first of its use as a metaphor at the urban scale by writers like Fred Koetter and Colin Rowe, who pointed to the traditional city's "solid and continuous matrix of texture" as a kind of "supporting ground" for the city and a counter to the idea of architecture as object. Although Koetter and Rowe rarely use texture alone, without other adjacent terms (matrix, ground) to support its meaning, they imply its definition as a background quality or characteristic encompassing both the material and the visual. Texture also frequently appears during the first half of the twentieth century in interiors magazines like *House Beautiful*, suggesting a relationship with decoration. This more active—or at least additive—role shares something with the image "texture maps" that were applied to early digital renderings in the 1990s.

Somewhere between these two views—texture-as-metaphor and texture-as-application—lies "Texture as a Visual Phenomenon," a 1963 *Architectural Design* article by César Jannello, then a professor of visual studies at the University of Buenos Aires. Jannello's analysis of texture relies on mathematical ratios and characteristics such as directionality, which inform our perception of a texture's appearance. His break-down of what makes texture legible is in direct response to what he sees as a lacuna in our understanding—a "conceptual incapacity" in the face of a phenomenon that compared to color, for example, is an "almost unexplored dominion." Today, Jannello's rule-based approach might easily lead to the intricate surface articulations of digital form, which is ironic given the flatness of texture maps in this context. But Jannello consciously avoids using texture as metaphor, abstract generative, or affective goal; for him, rather, "the significant role of texture consists in denoting the actual presence of the material." At the same time, each individual element composing a texture must subsume itself to the whole—what Jannello calls "textual significance" is a function of this operation. Here, texture is and is not what it is.

This brings us closer to what is specifically American—or at least to me, an American, and an admittedly confused and angry one at the moment—about texture in Paul's work, beyond hallways reminiscent of the south-suburban Chicago schools I attended in the 1990s. The negation/transubstantiation of the part to the whole is magical, but the identification with specific material realities is banal, and I see this split as a nice kind of American tradition. The commercial is always present in the US. We are not so elegant, and we are certainly not elegant enough to pull off minimalism, really. It is not that Main Street is almost all right but more that Main Street is so boring, so repeated everywhere, that it simply must become strange, like a word you say repeatedly that eventually loses its meaning. As Paul suggests, architects can find opportunity in this strangeness. Even more, at a time when we are living in constant awareness of seemingly unreconcilable extremes, to assert that something is not what it is in a generous, open way—even with the thing immediately in front of you—becomes a kind of essential cultural and even political responsibility. This quality is present in Paul's textures, and opens up more than what it is while remaining unmistakably what it is.

I realize it might seem naïve to argue for the fundamental importance of estrangement, of making the ordinary extraordinary, but here we are. We need to establish some common baselines for what we architecture people are doing.

One of Torres's pointed comments relates to his immigration status, defined by our government as an "alien with extraordinary ability." He makes light of the work he is doing in *My Favorite Shapes* as a form of labor, joking that he has stolen this particular job from an American. That Torres feels this country is a place where he can find what he is looking for, where he can work in this absurd way, gives me some faith. Architects need to work in this way, too. To paraphrase Torres talking to his mother before he materializes on stage at the beginning of the special, if we don't, then no one else would.

Birdwatchers and Trainspotters

Alex Lehnerer

It is relatively easy to understand why someone would play football, tennis, or chess: the physical activity, competition, and tension are exciting, entertaining things. It is less easy to understand why some of our contemporaries wait at railway embankments in their free time for scheduled trains to pass. These aren't historical locomotives passing by but rather the regional train on its daily route. It is an utterly normal scene. I don't mean the *Blue-Velvet*-normal of David Lynch, where the horror lurks under a conventionally pruned green turf—normality being an ingredient of the exciting, a stylistic device. But "normal" in the predictable, punctual, reliable, without incident, orderly sense.

Something is still strange here at the tracks. There is no depth, nothing hidden, nothing clandestine. Even the metaphysics of the timetable unfold in the usual way: felt with a slight crackling in the steel of the tracks, a swelling noise brought to a roar, grinding, slowing to a squeal, a draft, then silence again. It's the 17:05 regional train, RE 2403, from Bamberg to Nuremberg—one traction unit, a Siemens EuroSprinter ES64U2 Taurus, followed by 12 passenger cars. Next stop: Erlangen at 17:09—most likely on time. No secret, no ambiguity, no deviation from the rule, it is the reliable standard of the summer timetable. Nevertheless, some guy over there takes a photo and notes of the most normal thing in the world. I don't understand it, and that is exactly why it's fascinating. Not the scene itself—the banal, predictable event—but the person who is nevertheless interested in it. Why?

Paul Preissner is such a trainspotter. Although, if you asked him, he would try to convince you that he is more of a birdwatcher. Architects can easily be divided into these two hobby preferences. This is perhaps a rough generalization, like the hedgehog and the fox; we have so many examples, including the two antipodes of Isaiah Berlin handed down to the field of architecture by Colin Rowe in *Collage City*. Yet still, each of these juxtapositions is associated with a certain kind of insight.

Birdwatchers are not ornithologists, nor are trainspotters train conductors. On the contrary, their professional distance makes observing birds and trains a consciously exciting, intimate, and (above all) freeing experience. Architects have a similar amateur freedom as they are rarely construction workers. They are not artists either. Artists work directly on their piece; their hands-on process immediately manifests in the final product. Architects, on the other hand, always have the drawing between their artifact and themselves. They labor on the work's planning with more or less leeway. They preconceive, and are happy when things turn out as expected. They are the trainspotter, whose list simultaneously embodies his own forwarded expectation and the rearwarded control of others—calculation combined with measurement, speculation with empiricism.

Speculation as (re-)evaluation of the normal becomes the project. Birdwatchers don't typically observe spectacular animals; instead, the focus is on those animals at their front doorstep. Since they are commonly seen, robins do not have to be hunted with binoculars. An orange-red colors the forehead, throat, and front breast, while the upper tail blankets are a yellow-brown and the lower tail blankets a cream-color. As an important member of the flycatcher family, they are always worth the close look—not because you discover something special but because you find the familiar confirmed. The view through the binoculars is a benign form of appropriation: a brief, ephemeral framing of the familiar as a visual cut-out, an isolating act with a shallow depth of field. Thereby, birdwatchers resemble architects, in tracking down and reframing familiar forms.

Unfortunately, it is now increasingly clear to me that my idea of juxtaposing birdwatchers and trainspotters does not work so well after all. The big difference lies in the type of object under investigation (perhaps this is obvious). Some like trains, others like birds, so what? More interesting is the differentiation between passive and active behavior, the difference between waiting for the train and finding the bird. The latter provokes the possible surprise that beside the robin at the edge of the forest, the much rarer and endangered redstart can suddenly be seen. This would be spectacular. Yet this rare sighting isn't what Paul is after—at least not right now.

Stadt Zürich
Wasservögel

When I started writing this essay, the word "dumb" was used only once in *Kind Of Boring* and I began by pointing out that it was nonetheless crucial to understanding the book. By the time I finished, it was not only used all the times I use it but a "Dumb Manifesto" had become the climax of an essay Paul himself was writing. Which suggests that "dumb" does matter and turns my own "Dumb and Boring" into an effort, running parallel to his, to say what's at stake in making work that is convincingly described not only as dumb but as "boring," "messy", and "clumsy." After all, these adjectives are usually pejorative, and it's not like Paul Preissner is giving them some new, non-pejorative meanings. When he talks about the Port of Kinmen Ferry Terminal (2014) as consisting of "big dumb objects," he isn't using the word "dumb" to mean subtly expressive; he means they're inexpressive. And when he says about his work in general that it's "kind of just boring, somewhat messy, and aesthetically dumb,"[1] he doesn't mean that it's actually fascinating and secretly articulate. In fact, as the "kind of" that introduces boring and that gives this book its title suggests, a certain inarticulateness is essential to his work or at least, to its self-description.

At the same time, however, along with the messiness, there's a certain specificity to the work and especially, despite its dumbness, a certain kind of demand it makes. Right from the start, for example, the title *Kind Of Boring* is followed by a subtitle—"Canonical Work and Other Visible Things Meant to be Viewed as Architecture"—that tells us what the book will contain in a way that goes along with dumb ("Visible Things" is a description that barely describes) but that also instructs us in the kind of attention we're supposed to pay to them—it tells us how they're "meant." And although "kind of" sounds rhetorically imprecise, the assortment of the world into natural kinds (famous philosophical example: water) and the kinds of debate that assortment produces (classic question: is ice hardened water? Possible answers: yes, no, kind of.) may lead us to redescribe that imprecision as the fruit of intense attention.[2] So if, on the one hand, the visible things in this book are "kind of just boring," on the other hand, the boringness is less an invitation to pay no attention than a demand that we think about what it means for them to be boring, that we view them as they're "meant."

We can begin to get an idea of how this works by looking at Foam Thing (2015) ("thing" for Preissner is another almost technical term; this thing is "a dirtless pile of foam" made into "hillsides and towers"). Looking at the photos, what's striking is first, the degree to which the Thing becomes visible as what it is only when there are people using it and, second, how little difference it makes whether the people are real or just little figurines, how similar they are in their effect and even in their affect. This is not because the plastic figures are super realistic or psychologically compelling or in any way striking; on the contrary, they're just generic. But it's also not because the generic quality of the figurines is meant as a kind of ironic reflection on the generic character of real people. In other words, it's not a critique of dehumanizing capital on the model, say, of Malvina Reynolds's famous ballad of architectural conformism, criticizing the people "made out of ticky-tacky" who live in "the little boxes on the hill side," also "made of ticky-tacky" and who, just like the boxes, "all look just the same." For Preissner the proximity of the flesh and blood people to the painted plastic ones is an emblem of his work's unwillingness to demand a certain kind of attention. In fact, the plastic people demonstrate even better than the real ones how the Thing can be used without its being made into an object of aesthetic appreciation. We could almost say that their plasticness signifies their ability to withhold the attention that Preissner doesn't want to demand. In *Kind Of Boring*, it expresses the architects' desire (Preissner's and his partner on this and several other projects, Paul Andersen's) desire to leave them alone.

But to say that Foam Thing does not offer itself as an object of aesthetic appreciation is not to say that it doesn't have an aesthetic. It's to say instead what Preissner says of his work in general, that it's "aesthetically dumb." A lot of architecture doesn't want to leave people alone. In fact, it wants to do just the opposite. It wants to capture their attention and (often although not always) with the best motives in the world, to encourage them to behave in certain ways. In art, Michael Fried, following Diderot, has called this appeal to the beholder "theatricality" and the alternative to it "absorption."[3] The theatrical work of art performs for the beholder or seeks to involve her in the production of its meaning. The absorptive work—from, say, the portrait of a woman so intensely involved in her reading that she seems unaware she's being painted to the abstract painting that depicts only its relation to itself—makes the experience of the beholder irrelevant to its meaning.

This project of making the work indifferent to the beholder is literalized and in some ways intensified in photography. Just think of the lengths (Walker Evans on the subway with his concealed camera, Helen Levitt on the street with her right angle lens) to which photographers have gone to get pictures of people who are not performing for them and thus not performing for us and think of every photograph you've ever seen (or taken) in which the subject is posing, trying to look a certain way to produce a certain effect. (Of course, photographs of plastic people go a long way toward solving this problem.) But in architecture, where there really isn't any such thing as a beholder, that is, where the experience of the beholder is her experience of living in or working or meeting friends in the work, it's hard to see how you could or why you would even want to make the experience of the user irrelevant. Fried describes the project of absorption as one of overcoming the literal relation of the subject (beholder) to the object (the painting). On the one hand, the painting was made to be looked at and, if it's successful, is being looked at; on the other hand, the effort of the work was to ignore or overcome that fact, to establish its autonomy from the viewer. Buildings are even more literal than paintings — "irreducibly literal," as Colin Rowe and Robert Slutzky said in *Transparency: Literal and Phenomenal* (1964) even before Fried himself deployed "literal" as a (kind of) synonym for theatricality in "Art and Objecthood" (1967). They are made for people to use. How could you, why would you want to, what would it mean to overcome that?

Foam Thing provides some answers. A "dirtless pile of foam" made "into hillsides and towers," it is, Preissner says, "a new natural landscape." So, "like any hillside," it can offer an "enjoyable space" ("for recreation") or an "annoying" one (if you just want to get to the other side). What it doesn't do (what makes its foam more like nature than it is like "ticky-tack") is address itself to you. And in this respect it's different from what Preissner criticizes as the architectural effort to solicit our interest, different from what (in a memorable phrase) he calls the "creep of attention-capture." The idea here is that his own refusal to be interesting to (and to be interested in, except in the most generic way) the people who will use what he has made performs a double function. It establishes the autonomy of the work from their responses to it (there's a sense, fictional but important, in which it wasn't made for them). And it respects their autonomy; instead of demanding that they be fascinated by and responsive to the architecture, it provides them with a (utopian in concept but real in execution) space of their own.

So boring means what it usually does (not interesting) but not interesting means not that you can't be interested in it but that it doesn't demand your interest. And dumb means not telling you what to do or how to feel, which (when followed by indifferent, as in "kind of just boring, somewhat messy, and aesthetically dumb, and indifferent") means not only not telling you what to do but also not caring what you do.

But Preissner doesn't just want indifferent, boring, and dumb—he wants "aesthetically" dumb. So what's added by aesthetic? Foam Thing is "like" nature; it doesn't have any designs on you. But it's not nature; it has meaning—it's "meant to be viewed as architecture." And to see something as architecture is, as Preissner has said elsewhere, to see in it the "form of the work."[4] The point

is that in nature things can be boring and dumb but in architecture, boring and dumb are formal characteristics. Aesthetically dumb is thus not quite the same as dumb; aesthetically dumb architecture not only leaves you alone but must be understood as leaving you alone. In architectural terms, we can see a version of this distinction in the difference articulated in the Rowe and Slutzky essay mentioned above, between "literal" transparency (like glass walls, which give you the physical ability to see something behind something else) and what they call "phenomenal" transparency, which produces what they characterize as the implication of a third dimension without actually or necessarily showing it. In other words, it's one thing for something to be transparent; it's another for it to represent transparency. When a surface just is transparent, we can see through it; when it also represents transparency, we need to understand what it means to see through it.

So what's added by aesthetic is what it means not just to do what a hillside does—make no demands—but to do what no hillside can do –be about making no demands. That is, aesthetically dumb architecture doesn't demand anything from you both because it doesn't try to provoke you into a response and because what it does instead is ask you to understand the meaning of its refusal to provoke. And it's that understanding which is not only at the heart of the form of the work but of what Preissner in the same talk called the "politics" of that form. Understanding is at the heart of form because the form of the work—let's say the fact that to understand Foam Thing is to understand that it's meant to be "like" a hillside—is to acknowledge the difference between what it is and how we respond to it, a difference that Preissner's commitment to "indifference" doubles down on. Why? Because what he wants is work that is indifferent in two senses: first, as we have seen, it doesn't seek to produce a response in us; second, it means what it means regardless of what our response is. In other words, it's indifferent both affectively and logically. We might say here that that if the value of the first kind of indifference is that it leaves us room to feel for ourselves (Preissner likes to call this "daydreaming"), the value of the second is that it leaves us room to think for ourselves.

But this understates the importance of the logical claim. Foam Thing is a piece of public architecture and its insistence on its form is a way of describing the public it imagines (and thereby seeks to help create). The kind of architecture that Preissner is objecting to—interesting rather than boring, seeking to produce an effect –imagines its public as the people upon whom the effect is (or is not) produced. By contrast, dumb architecture's indifference to the question of how people respond to it imagines a public constituted by how they understand (or misunderstand) it. And it's this conception of the public that leads Preissner to think of his commitment to a dumb aesthetics as also a commitment to a class politics. Instead of being structured like a market, understood in terms of differing consumer preferences, it's structured ideologically—by the potential for conflict that's concealed when represented as patterns of consumption (I'm bored, you're not) but insisted upon when it's understood as interpretive: we don't just differ, we disagree.

In fact, of course, underlying both the market and the public square is the conflict that makes both possible—class conflict. But the appeal of architecture as commodity redescribes it as a hierarchy of taste while the dumb aesthetic, making the potential for conflict intrinsic to it, makes the actuality of conflict visible beneath it, not that either the painted figures or the real ones anywhere in this book look like they're about to declare class war. What Preissner depicts here is the capacity for a class politics, egalitarian not in the meritocratic sense of "to each according to his ability" but more like the famous alternative. If, then, part of the appeal of the many photographed, modeled, and digitized people in this book is their inexpressiveness—our sense that their interior lives are theirs—another part of the appeal is their universality—our sense that their lives could be anyone's. So it's no surprise that the actual word "egalitarian" is one that Preissner likes almost as much as he likes dumb and boring or that one of the times it's invoked here is in connection with his effort (Port of Kinmen Ferry

Terminal, 2014) to introduce "the concept of big dumb objects as an approach to removing the personal or emotional distance created by the scale of large infrastructural buildings." It's the dumbness that removes the distance; the "personal" relation it establishes is the relation of anyone to anyone (the possibility of solidarity). It's the "concept" of dumbness that turns that personal relation (a kind of identification) into the impersonal one of agreement. Concepts need to be understood, and the solidarity of a class politics involves not just belonging to a class but organizing around the idea (the concept) of class conflict. The Ferry Terminal is designed to "allow egalitarian access to the water"; the big dumb buildings that make this access possible mark also the ambition to make it general, to make egalitarianism into a principle as well as a physical fact.

Which brings us back to "kind of." "Kind of" means "fuzzy" (another word Preissner likes), as if the boundaries between one thing and another were so blurry that you couldn't quite tell one from another. But in fact there's no "kind of" without kinds, no kinds without a concept. So this whole book is written under the sign of the concept. It's almost as if it were addressed to the Lenin who, after he started reading Hegel, famously wrote that "intelligent idealism is closer to intelligent materialism than stupid materialism."[5] Of course, "stupid" is one definition of dumb, but, as we've seen, the essence of the dumb in *Kind Of Boring* is already ideal. What Hegel gave Lenin was a better sense of the dialectic, of the relation between the material and the idea. What a dialectical architecture would look like is hard to say (and I'm pretty sure the Kinmen Ferry Terminal project was not designed after a few days reading the *Science of Logic*). But it's in big dumb objects like those ferry buildings that the stupidity of materialism begins its transformation into an idealism that would no longer be just the opposite of meterialism but might instead turn out to be a kind of materialism.

Thanks to Jennifer Ashton and Todd Cronan for equally (but differently) essential help with this essay.

1 Paul Preissner, "A Letter to Andrew Holder," *Fresh Meat Journal*, August 2016, www.freshmeatjournal.com/pau.

2 John Locke, *An Essay Concerning Human Understanding* (London: 1689).

3 Michael Fried, *Absorption and Theatricality: Painter and Beholder in the Age of Diderot* (Chicago: University of Chicago Press, 1980).

4 Paul Preissner, "(Low-resolution Houses Symposium Day 2)," Low-Resolution Houses Symposium, Princeton University School of Architecture, [November 9, 2018], [14:52], https://vimeo.com/showcase/5588105/video/303353356

5 Vladimir Ilyich Lenin, "Conspectus of Hegel's Book *Lectures on the History of Philosophy*," in *Collected Works*, vol. 38, 4th ed., trans. Clemence Dutt, ed. Stewart Smith (Moscow: Progress, 1976), 269–300, https://www.marxists.org/archive/lenin/works/1914/cons-logic/ch03.htm.

Kind of Boring

Paul Preissner

There are a lot of pictures and images to look at in the world now thanks to the cultural clearinghouse of the internet and social media, books, magazines, and friends. Some are spectacular, some are gross, some are funny, most are ordinary, and some are pretty boring. This firehose of visual culture captures most of my attention, and as I've entered my forty-fifth year looking at things my eyes get a little glossy at interesting things. Where the novel and saturated picture used to occupy my mind for long periods of time, I now find more enjoyment, depth, and attraction with the boring and mundane things. Part of this is exhaustion, I suppose, but another reason is that there is somehow more feeling and complexity in the depictions of the weird parts of the world. The wonderful is obvious and remarkable, but it's also known and knowable. There's no wilderness to the spectacle and no confusion with novelty. Those things are immediate and "speak" to us. The interesting aptly communicates what it is, and as a viewer, I like it or don't, but there isn't much room for thought, just appreciation. The boring offers more space for thought, or even more space to drift. It doesn't always have a point, or even a comment. It's a nebulous body of things that often confuses and makes one curious about motive or composition or points.

Perhaps the underlying problem with the interesting (or at least the reason for my lessening of interest in the interesting) is that it works within the conservative model of "taste." You can like it, or not, but that feeling reflects whether you accept or reject its extension of an established cultural project. There seems to be no model allowing one's indifference about interesting things. There is a belief about "taste" that it's a real thing, and that, more than it just being an existential characteristic or quality one might "have," it is in some way evidence of some intellectual or moral superiority an individual possesses. That it is often just accepted without much examination seems to only serve the status quo interests of the generationally wealthy and powerful. This existence in the world of distinction and efforts to constantly capture our attention (through our eyes) tend to make us unfree.

Boring things open the world up. There is no request for attention or need for applause or approval. It's boring. It's already something with little (initially) to offer. Boring and dull things are empty. However, it's this void that allows for things which are normal, anonymous, and quotidian to become weird and strange and make space for the imagination. It's a free space in all the ways that interesting things are a closed room.

Anyhow, no one knows what anything is anymore. The idea of there being any sort of coherent field of architecture disappeared shortly after information became a consumable object. Architecture became a solvable problem that parametric tools could give us the complete models to understand and optimize. Aesthetics could be freed from politics and opinion and handed off to the discrete curves of calculus.

None of the architectural promises from the past seem to have really made anything better for everyone. There's a lot of bizarre things around now, and they all seem expensive and only sometimes well done. They also all kind of feel like successes that benefit only a really tiny amount of people, often at the debasement and expense of large populations of other people. It's hard to feel really optimistic or confident about the future, which makes for kind of a weird anxiety about the architectural present. What is it? It's no longer clear where it's going and even less clear now where it's come from.

It's difficult to imagine any kind of original architecture at this point. Architecture has never been less certain. That the stakes are often described as never having been higher should be the tell that they are perhaps quite historically low. When everything is urgent, nothing is important. When nothing is important, everything becomes a magnetic north of its own.

Architecture became closed at the exact moment it mastered being interesting. Spectacular architecture has been a goal in the field and the academy for so long that its own set of rules, tricks, and best practices developed. Technology replaced ideas. The fuzzy overlap of the art market and easy money made its funding doable enough to make it happen enough to make it no longer so special. For every Guggenheim, there are three more Guggenheims. Everything is so complex now, so on-demand, and parametrically controlled from mine to skyscraper. No geometry is impossible and no expenses spared. Hats can only release so many doves before you long for when they simply contained one's dandruff. That kind of thing.

But this intensification of effect, expense, immediacy, and urgency also suggests an escape path: indifference, carelessness, normalcy, and dumbness. Architecture has developed into a new market commodity no different than the smart thermostats specified to sit on its walls and spy on its inhabitants. Social space is no longer well served by architecture; it's too prescribed and prescriptive. We are told the future is smart cities and smarter buildings, but all we really want is to be left alone in peace for a few spare minutes. Special no longer surprises. Interesting is just exhausting. When the world is full of originals, being normal is the scariest form of expression.

Being dumb exposes the disposability of uniqueness.

Dumb space is the rejection of the fringe, which is oddly crowded. Having mastered spectacle, dumb space turns attention toward mastering sameness. Dumb space finds the suburbs more compelling than the "city." It confuses big and small, lets the most minor of parts play leads, and gives the largest profile the more trivial tasks. Dumb space is the vaguely familiar and contains a lot of things that by themselves are entirely unremarkable and even super common to the degree that you don't even question their authority. Yet they don't seem to be quite right, or the same as you remember them, but then again you can't quite recall how they were before anyhow, since even back then they were only the smallest of things, with no real importance and certainly no significance. Dumb space is a fit that is both too roomy and oddly confining. It's the space of choice. It's a construction of a rejection of the state of the world and a decision to create a new one without bothering to replace the details. Dumb space is a colony of things that don't belong together but don't necessarily not belong together either. You don't really know. It doesn't feel right, but it feels more right than you've felt in a long time. Dumb space is the suspicion of obligation. It's the freedom to be inactive. It's an inert request. Dumb space thinks the wall is just as important as the door and wonders if the coat hook is actually a king. Dumb space creates room for careless combinations and new architecture with minimal effort. Dumb space looks for noodles, gets thrilled by squiggles, and allows for things to get weird. Dumb space isn't nostalgic for an excavated past or fixated on distant technological future. Dumb space is pretty happy with later this afternoon. Dumb space is so normal and pragmatic. Architecture is more interesting when its not entirely clear where the effort exists.

Anyhow, no one can afford boring anymore. A long time ago, if you bought generic or lesser quality, it meant you were subjected to generic or lesser quality design, meaning thought and effort. This meant things or spaces were unadorned, undecorated, and more or less looked like the most pragmatic version of that thing possible. If you weren't rich, your kid's toys, your toaster, or whatever, was guaranteed to be bland, dull, boring, empty, and without refined detail, decoration, or material variety. At some point that changed (probably around the mid-1970s, since I can remember some pretty boring toys and things early in my childhood and a clear lack of them in later parts of childhood). And the ease of manufacturing and the expansion of inexpensive material possibilities meant that clutter became common. Variety was introduced as a universal positive, and combinations of shape, materials, and spaces were given to everyone at every scale.

There are no boring toys at Target.

For dull toys one needs to go to Galt Baby. What was once the only choice for those of fewer means has become out of reach for most, as everyone except for the rich have no choice but to live interesting, saturated, visually busy lives. Boringness, it turns out, is a luxury.

To return to the problem of the world of interesting things, there is no space inside. It is suffocating. All oxygen is consumed by the object or architecture "expressing itself" at volume. I get a headache. Dumbness gets that being left alone and daydreaming feels much better than seeing things perform. Dumbness also gets that perfect and clean is just as awful as interesting but perhaps at the opposite side of terrible, since it condescends about order.

Fuzziness and awkward positions make for an architecture that levels a critique against architecture of expense through finding a way to be complex without money.

To this end, architecture has sort of found itself stuck in a trap as of late. Whereas the normalizing regulations that are zoning and building codes have produced a world that either looks to replicate the status quo and express normalcy, or imagine itself as misbehaving and produce some form of specialness. This gives us a world in which architecture finds itself to only have these two options either being some version of monument or else, existing as the crowd. Dumbness is a belief in architecture to also be not-normal but also not-special, a kind of fuzzy thing that seems both straight and crooked simultaneously. This is confusing if only because staring never seems to make the thing clearer. The desire for monumentality or context both fail the world because they exist in a very conservative moral code of the individual. In architecture as it's stuck today there can be no other manner of existence, and the result of this is a vanity fair of novelty, expressions of wealth, expressions of modesty, expressions of morality, and peacock-like demonstrations of individuality in which someone doesn't resist the world they pretend to be against, but simply celebrates the cultural hierarchy of material. Architecture either subjugates the ego or permits expressions of it, but there is never anything weird about anything anymore, and the wild investigations into novelty feel as flat and soulless as the flat and soulless mediocrity they claim to escape from. Both are morally identical in their mapping of an architectural ambition to the imagined possible roles of the human ego, and this replication of ambition (even if the product is superficially at odds) reduces architecture to a trivial object regardless of its actual design.

This is the circumstance that the built world has constructed for itself, and it's evidenced through the objectification of architecture in the public arena, as well as the education of the architect in the institution. Students are taught to either stand out with some formal invention or to "contribute to the betterment of the planet" through their ego suppression and acceptance of whatever cause-de-jour of the profession (green technology, new urbanism morality, contextualism, low-cost low-idea housing, etc). I think this ends up confirming the worst stereotype of architecture and condemns it to operating in the world in a single, uninteresting way: every project is in the end just a reflection of a person. Architecture is only able to operate as art, and should only be appreciated as art object. This goes back to relying on some strata of taste, which is always in the service of money. But this super-conscious operation as some kind of art object is producing the most obnoxious forms of architecture. All fluffed up by production tricks, today's architecture works so hard trying to come off as free and radical, new, and wild, but all that I see is the labor behind it. And this is not in some cool, self-aware, Marxist way. The complicated metaphors and geometries do not seem to demonstrate some effortless mastery of architecture, but just affectation: all decorative and subsumed by a clear ambition to signify elite notions of what is provocative. But this kind of provocation never actually makes anyone uncomfortable or reflects the world, it just makes people either like it or not like it or whatever. Who even cares? Next week there will be a new new thing to look at. This kind of architecture is entertainment for the bored affluent, not art. I get that that's also historically and traditionally what architecture always was and who architecture has always kind of been for (even the most generous reading of mid-century modernism and its for-the-people kind of nobility still has to confront the reality that at that moment in time the people in its for-the-people-ness was pretty narrowly confined to white men) but that's perhaps why I find this contemporary posturing of architecture and its authors so cloying and offensive. All the signifiers of rebellion have become clichés of conformity, giving us nothing less than a clear demonstration of neoliberal postmodernism's ultimate political victory.

So this is where we are collectively. This is a bit of a bummer and perhaps why the architecture project of today, in its quest to be interesting and its posturing as provocation, produces average architectural space and in general seems simply like a distraction. Interestingness isn't a necessary condition of architecture.

Space is much better when it's extremely, super normal or kind of almost normal, or mostly normal. The vaguely familiar forms of architecture give space for things to be uncanny and odd and in the end, to make people reflective on the world and what architecture says about that world. Architecture should be weird, create weak form, and develop a strange social space. When it's trying to be interesting, it is just not very interesting, and worse, it is simply reinforcing the self-conception of the upper classes of the world that they are the chosen stewards of taste and judgement.

We are surrounded by buildings that are immediately clear in their purpose and targets. They often do something for you, like keep the rain away, or move shoppers through quickly and lucratively, or just demand attention and awe. Architecture today rarely turns out to be our friend.

It's through making the normal weird that architecture has the chance to offer motivation and not just conditioning, to be an open question rather than a finite object. If the city is the one big project of society, architecture can be its black hole, allowing for the projection of make-believe and the curiosity of indeterminate purpose. And to conclude (or at least to wrap it up), this black hole of work seemingly requires the privileging of the world of normal, anonymous, weird, strange things over the interesting, using the project of pictures, memes, and images as a carefree form of precedent of spirit to allow a relaxed idea of precision and composition to enter the architectural project.

A Very Brief Note on Music

Li Tavor

Composer Mauricio Kagel once wrote a musical series of marches for woodwind, brass, and percussion titled *10 Märsche um den Sieg zu Verfehlen* ("10 Marches to Miss the Victory").[1] Kagel, who was born in Argentina into a Jewish-Russian family during the Second World War, was highly dedicated to any musical practice of contradictory and anti-ideological nature, as exemplified in his 1978 march series. His sensibility for images—meaning the representational value of cultural significance and collective memory—within musical form is most visible in the march compositions.

Historically, forms of marching music existed in ancient Greece, but its cultural significance grew around the turn of the twentieth century, when it was used as a form of representation for the military to demonstrate its decency, to get a group of bodies—mainly within a corps—to march in lockstep, in order to reach a desired territory as quick as possible. March music is a highly repetitive form with straightforward rhythms and melodies, demonstrated by its simple time metric. In fact, the musical language of a march is so ordinary that most listeners disregard its structure immediately. Because it was the only music broadcasted through the radio in the 1940s, march music was huge in wartime Germany and could closely be described as the pop music of this national moment—even though pop music had yet to be born and certainly would not have originated in Germany (Adorno would hate this comparison).

Concurrently, during and after World War II, Austria and Germany were hot spots for new and experimental music in Europe. Kagel was without a doubt one of a few very important figures within these developments, having moved to Germany in 1957. One of the goals of this new music was to move away from the images, forms, and techniques of the past, toward a new understanding of structure, form, language, sound morphologies, and production techniques. Rhetorics were no longer generated through studies of poetic figures but through mathematics, new technological inventions, and a new understanding of time and space relations. This modernist rigour was driven by the so called "Darmstädter Ferienkurse," where every important figure in the music scene—

including Kagel—met every two years to discuss and exercise the novelties of contemporary music. Kagel experimented with every possible new technique, material, and medium: radio, oscillators, filters, noise, serial techniques, you name it, but always with a self-critical eye on his colleagues and his own euphoric search for new form. Interestingly enough, he was one of the few composers that didn't shy away from acknowledging that certain historical and traditional references can and must be used as effective material for new developments of musical thoughts, however problematic the precedent material may be.

Kagel's social commentary further disclosed his position within a milieu of insiders and fellow composers at the time. Avant-garde composers often kept a healthy distance from mainstream musical audiences. Yet Kagel seemingly moved towards the masses, the normal, and the ordinary. It enabled him to create irritation and differences within patterns of habitual behaviors. For its time, Kagel's crude appropriation of the march was counterintuitive and forced postwar audiences to reflect on the recent past. With *10 Märsche um den Sieg zu Verfehlen*, he challenged the weighty societal meaning of marching music to make every existing German pacemaker strumble for a second. This disorientating moment was dedicated to every citizen who sat in their homes thirty years prior, listening to the single radio frequency broadcasted in Germany, matching the rhythm of each march with their own heartbeat. His marches musically demonstrated how easily certainties can derail. Through subtle moves, like syncopation and shifts of timbres, the music manages to constantly shoot itself in the foot. Sometimes the entire brass ensemble falls apart in a fit of leaden fatigue, the trumpets lose their momentum, or the trombone plods lonely into the void with a clumsy melody.[2] Even though the rhythmic structures of the various arrangements may seem as simple as the original march, the time metrics become so complex that only very skilled instrumentalists are able to play them. This organized chaos is further amplified by an ensemble that is purposefully out of tune, because Kagel's instructions explain that the instruments should not be tuned at all.

Upon listening to *10 Märsche um den Sieg zu Verfehlen*, my first reaction was laughter. It's funny to understand how easy it is to use dumb, unagitated musical material and turn it into something that feels very wrong without understanding why. After thinking about the arrangement for a while, my laughter turned into melancholy. Then I laughed again because Kagel brilliantly subverted the boring "uff-ta uff-ta uff-ta-ta-ta" march as a musical form. This new form becomes something playful to fantasize and speculate on as an image of political and military power, a medium of propaganda, and an object of collective memory. Disarming the hidden and destructive purpose of marches, Kagel's composition visualizes the invisible complexity of an ordinary object through an effortless, almost marginal appearance.
I wish buildings could be a bit more like that.

1 *March No. 4* is my favorite; to listen, go to www.youtube.com/watch?v=wJYtJyP0HU4

2 Claus Spahn, "On the Death of Mauricio Kagels, Who Was Much More than a Composer," *Die Zeit* 40 (September 25, 2008), https://www.zeit.de/2008/40/Nachruf-Kagel.

Kind of Some General Practices for a Dumb Manifesto

Paul Preissner

These are some of what is thought about when making this work and are also some of the things talked about when talking about making architecture and is maybe more generally how we go about doing our work.

1 If being visually special is a way of grabbing attention, it's also a way of being incredibly obnoxious. It's perhaps better to introduce the strange feeling of something being weirdly familiar and not at all obviously new.

2 There shouldn't be much thought put towards coherence. There are only our projects. They don't relate to many other projects, but they do share some things like doors; walls, columns, windows, and other "elements"; and colors. There are floors and other things that look like architecture but most important for the work is that you can walk into them and they mostly make practical sense.

3 Architecture is generally pretty complicated and the less the project looks like an object design thought experiment, the better. We probably resolved its space and purpose.

4 Be more boring. Spend more time trying to be really, remarkably normal.

5 Details are details. They don't need be perfect or remarkable. Having a relaxed attitude toward this obsession of the practice gives the work a greater feeling of the wilderness a project has. Most materials have edges not intended for people to see, but those are the most emotional edges to look at. Don't cover those up.

6 There's a spirit to dumbness that is a kind of rejection of monied tastes and preferences. Explore the pleasure, details, and architecture that comes through confusion over whether something is good, incompetent, weird, or normal. We're not quite sure which one is us.

7 There isn't any real ownership to these ideas, and these experiments, compositions, or expressions shouldn't produce some proprietary form of architecture, just general ideas for everyone.

8 Some things are just cheap. Those are the best things.

9 Weak colors are better. Normal beiges, delivery-service browns, maybe peach and possibly a dusty sky blue and then mustard and common lake green are really just wonderful colors. So are white grey and dust. If the colors feel right right away they're probably the wrong ones to use anyhow.

10 When there's a choice, always pick the poor one. There's more room for people in an architecture that seems a bit slow, and there's more room for politics in an architecture that is comfortable with being awkward.

11 Finally, generally, if the client says they want something, go ahead and give it to them, especially if it somehow feels totally out of place with whatever we've put together as the general project idea, and really messes up everything we've worked toward. The more causal collaboration that occurs, and more indifference enacted, the lighter and wilder the resulting project. We're interested in an architecture that is somewhat more carefree and unconcerned than most. It's not.

Special Economic Zone
Tripoli, Lebanon
60,000 sf
Design Team: Paul Preissner, David Ramis

This is a building development project for offices and housing in Tripoli, Lebanon on an old site being redeveloped into a new business district with housing for researchers. It's part of the exhibition site originally designed by the Brazilian architect Oscar Niemeyer. So our proposal somewhat addresses that particular form of concrete form and space through using the material in a very straightforward way that considers architecture as a very simple practice of placing things on top of other things until a building is produced. Precast components are oversized to enable hasty stacking, therefore ensuring that the resulting buildings are always slightly unstraight, both looking like what it is and making clear what it is: a very proper scheme that just mirrors the footprints of the two existing buildings and encourages a relaxed attitude towards social space.

House in Oregon
Oregon, Illinois
2,600 sf House
Design Team: Paul Preissner, David Ramis
Engineering: Goodfriend Magruder Structure, Yagla Engineering Services

This is a small house in the woods on a big property by a river in the middle of the upper part of Illinois. It's very plain and uses ground-faced concrete blocks to hold up quite a big roof. The house is square. The house has twelve windows, which also are all doors. There are two bedrooms and a good amount of social space for the family. This house will be the first building constructed as part of a long ambition of several other campground-like pavilions, structures, guest suites, and swimming and leisure things. The roof is made of fiber-reinforced corrugated cement panels.

Ring of Hope
Chicago, Illinois
24,000 sf Community Outreach and Youth Sports Center
Design Team: Paul Preissner, David Ramis
Engineering: Goodfriend Magruder Structure

Located at the intersection of three roads, two railways, and one interstate highway, the Ring of Hope is a community boxing and outreach center. The various programs of the building—boxing, cooking, eating, learning, training, exhibition, social, accommodation, fitness, competition, gardening, meditation—are separated into three levels and set on a public plaza at an intersection. It will create an open community space, linking the activities of the center with the daily life of the surrounding neighborhood. The drawings and representations of this project are to be considered in-progress.

DAR Al Uloum Library
Sakaka, Saudi Arabia
8,600 sm Library Renovation
Design Team: Paul Preissner, David Ramis

This competition entry is a renovation to an existing library from the 1960s that divided the symmetry of the plan into two identical libraries for separation of the genders. The new organization mixes gender and organizes the ground flood around a sunken lecture hall, exhibition spaces, and youth activities. The mezzanine volume connects these functions to the traditional library, which is indirectly illuminated by a staggered grid of solar chimneys. On top of the building is a newly constructed bar housing educational, meeting, and prayer rooms. The ground floor and all newly built portions use a metal solar screen to diffuse the sun and allow for a fully glazed space to not suffer the consequences of its openness. The campus is redesigned with a messy arrangement of shading elements producing a garden in the desert.

Liz and Morris House
Chicago, Illinois
3,000 sf House
Design Team: Ryan Hernandez, Paul Preissner
Engineering: Yagla Engineering Services
Photographs: Chris Strong

This is a house built for a family of six in a community between the North Branch of the Chicago river and the northern city limits of Chicago. The house is kind of a cube but with a slightly sloped roof running across the front elevation of the house. The home is an experiment in removing domestic features. The front of the house is partially covered in charred wood. The rest of the house is generically white, including the roof. The entrance is recessed, large, and glass. An equally sized interior corridor connects the front yard directly to the rear yard, collapsing space, while the double height kitchen and family room connect the living spaces to the floor of bedrooms.

1824–22
Chicago, Illinois
3,200 sf Apartment Building Renovation
Design Team: Ryan Hernandez, Paul Preissner
Engineering: Yagla Engineering Services
Photographs: Paul Preissner

This apartment project is a renovation of an unremarkable, except for its extreme normalcy, late nineteenth century Chicago paired two-flat. The building had been renovated a number of times in its past, with original window openings filled in and new openings cut out. New windows in deep steel boxes replaced the previous, and reveal the history of modifications which took place through the exposed casual patterns of Chicago common, buried limestone sills, and bricked-in openings of the past. A series of globe lights give a casual graphic pattern to the building front. This treatment of object windows and awkward lighting act as a form of historic preservation to call attention to the material history of modification of a very normal building. The interiors of the units are open and empty, allowing flexibility for the modest living space. Unit entries sit at the line between bedrooms and every other room, providing a social choice upon entrance. The decks overlook and provide access to a shared single yard.

Five Rooms
Chicago, Illinois
2,000 sf Gallery Installation
Design Team: Paul Andersen, Paul Preissner
Engineering: Goodfriend Magruder Structure
Photographs: James Florio, Tom Harris

The Chicago Cultural Center building was renovated in the 1970s to extend and transform the old public library into its new configuration. Merging a building that was designed for the distribution and storage of books with other civic functions left many interstitial spaces—like the Landmark Gallery—to suffer from an ambiguous identity as both gallery and corridor. It is too wide to be a hallway and too narrow to comfortably view exhibitions. One of several site-specific commissions for the 2017 Chicago Architecture Biennial, Five Rooms created a sequence of small galleries to house works selected by Jesús Vassallo as part of the photographic exhibition *A Love of the World*. The new rooms are defined by four pairs of heavy walls with curious stepped forms that reach toward the ramp overhead; they are made of structural glazed tile—a material commonly used in train stations, public schools, recreation centers, and other municipal buildings—in brick red and beige. The unconventional use of tile and the enfilade layout, which has been a defining form of museums and urban thoroughfares for centuries, sharpens the gallery's unique convergence of fine art and public works.

Big Apartment Complex
Tinley Park, Illinois
360,000 sf 300-Unit Apartment Complex, Retail and Parking
Design Team: Paul Preissner

This is an apartment complex for a development site in the downtown of Tinley Park, Illinois. The project consists of three courtyard buildings containing 300 apartments. The population is expected to be primarily divorced parents, who will use the apartments as residences to spend time with their children during weekends or the during the week. To this end each apartment is designed for use as a periodic family social space, rather than a place to store a household of goods. The design allows for a large courtyard to bring light, air, and views to the interior corridors through entire facades of glass. The exterior of the block-long building reduces the imposition of its size by loosening volumes and periodically introducing double height spaces with retail at the ground level near the commuter rail station. The unit volumes move in and out to provide a vibrated plan shape that allows for a few differing sizes of plans and create a much less monolithic chunk on the earth.

Pyeongchang-dong Art Complex
Seoul, South Korea
5,100 sm Four-Site Art Complex
Design Team: Paul Adjokun, Paul Preissner, Isabelle Redford

This complex distributes art exhibition, artist workshop, community education, and creative foundation offices across multiple sites on a steep terrain at the base of a moderate mountain near a nice river. The buildings fit the terrain though applied cubic volumes. Given the program, the cube was used as an anti-expressive form that lacks any aggression, implies no motion, and seems to be the least emotive shape. This serves as the basic element for the more thoughtful and emotive functions contained within. Each room is a raw interior, given character only by the exposed local stones embedded in the built and the art or activity taking place within.

Aarhus School of Architecture
Aarhus, Denmark
10,000 sm School of Architecture
Design Team: Paul Preissner

This is the concept for the new Aarhus School of Architecture building. Two horseshoe plan buildings holding lived towers provide the linear studio space that contains shared resources of libraries, seminar rooms and offices, as well as give boundary to social courtyards and the school canteen. There are no windows on the exterior of the project, only windows on the interior.

Apartment 2
Chicago, Illinois
1,800 sf Renovation of Upper 2-Bedroom Flat
Design Team: Ryan Hernandez, Paul Preissner
Photographs: Paul Preissner

This project is the complete redesign of the top flat of a two-flat building in one of Chicago's historic summer retreats for the rich during the nineteenth century, Edgewater. The layout and finishes reflect an attitude of openness, strange attractions, and colorfulness. The pairing of clumsy details with luxurious materials, or sometimes pretty cheap ones with perfect detailing, expresses an egalitarian and communal notion of life. The lighting is blunt, geometric, and loose throughout the kitchen, dining, and bathrooms and uses rather normal fixtures.

Summer Vault
Chicago, Illinois
200 sf Chicago Park District Lakefront Retail Kiosk
Design Team: Paul Andersen, Paul Preissner
Engineering: Goodfriend Magruder Structure
Photographs: Paul Andersen, Paul Preissner

Made in collaboration with the University of Illinois at Chicago, this is a lakefront kiosk that accommodates a multitude of things. It consists of basic geometric shapes—a twelve-foot-diameter barrel vault, a parallelogram, triangles—combined to create a curious, freestanding hang- out within the park. The interior of the skewed vault is divided into two triangular spaces—one enclosed by expanded metal screens and doors, and one open to the air but still within the vaulting. This two-part plan allows for commerce and community to occur simultaneously. It also reflects the kiosk's Persian origins as a thirteenth-century garden pavilion, while embracing its contemporary use as a seasonal commercial front and festive park retreat. Its openness allows year-round use so that it remains active even in its retail slumber during the Chicago winter.

Foam Thing
Denver, Colorado
2,000 sf Biennial of the Americas Pavilion
Design Team: Paul Andersen, Paul Preissner
Photographs: Paul Preissner

Geo-foam blocks are often stuffed inside the earth to create artificial landscape mounds and parklands without the added weight that comes with soil. We made a dirtless pile of foam into hillsides and towers for inside the principal event space for the 2015 Biennial of the Americas in Denver, Colorado, creating a new natural landscape. Like any hillside, these things provide enjoyable space for recreation and gathering and are also a little bit annoying when one is simply trying to walk to the other side.

Bamiyan Cultural Center
Bamiyan, Afghanistan
2,200 sm Cultural Center, Exhibition, Workshops, Performance Hall
Design Team: Jesus Corral, Paul Preissner

This building is a community art center, meeting hall, social space, and tourist destination for visitors to the region. The Bamiyan Cultural Center is in Afghanistan overlooking the World Heritage property of the giant mountain-carved Bamiyan Buddhas, which were demolished by the Taliban in 2001. Through a single level planning strategy of stone construction, the educational, expressive, research, administrative, cultural, performance, curatorial, and social events all take place within a connected ribbon of circulation separated by partitions without corners, allowing both privacy and lateral passage. Instead of creating a stylistic icon, this proposal offers a plan organization and building strategy that encourages more freedom of use, and allows for an architecture to develop a sense of politics about culture and its history, present. and future.

Apartment 1A
Chicago, Illinois
1,800 sf Combination and Renovation of Two Condo Units.
Design Team: Brett Gustafson, Paul Preissner
Photographs: Alan Froberg

A renovation combining two apartments in Hyde Park's tallest residential tower. The building names its unit types after famous Chicago architects, without having anything of substance within each apartment to tie it to those branded references. In this spirit, we combined an "Adler" and a "Mies van der Rohe" apartment together to discover a new form of unidentifiable history. We called this new type the Jahn.

Port of Kinmen Passenger Ferry Terminal
Kinmen, Taiwan
42,000 sm Passenger Terminal (Arrival/Departure), Port Service Center
Design Team: Jesus Corral, Julia Di Castri, Brett Gustafson, Paul Preissner

This is a port center and passenger terminal for a small island of Taiwan off the coast of China. The project is an experiment in buildings as a composition of oversized plain shapes and proposes a democracy of function within. The terminal sits directly on the earth and allows for direct approach, with one concourse element lifted to allow egalitarian access to the water. The architecture is simple and accessible and introduces the concept of big dumb objects as an approach to removing the personal or emotional distance created by the scale of large infrastructural buildings.

Image Index

1 Jessie Edelman at Andrew Rafacz Gallery by Paul Preissner Architects, 2020 by Ian Vecchiotti
2 Photo of motorcyclist in Havana, Cuba, 2017 by Paul Preissner
3 Photo of landfill construction, 1968 by Edgar Preissner
4 American Framing Pavilion Model, 2019 by Paul Andersen and Paul Preissner
5 City County Building Plaza rendering, 2014 by Paul Andersen and Paul Preissner
6 Jessie Edelman at Andrew Rafacz Gallery by Paul Preissner Architects, 2020 by Ian Vecchiotti
7 Belgian Garden Hedges by Daniel Ost
8 House in Quidi Vidi, 2018 by Paul Preissner
9 Picture of pink bathroom from the Internet
10 Katherine Lanski study model, 2018
11 Picture of the sea from the Internet
12 Jessie Edelman at Andrew Rafacz Gallery by Paul Preissner Architects, 2020 by Ian Vecchiotti
13 Picture of Toast Hawaii from the Internet
14 Picture of girl with ice cream cone in her nose from the Internet
15 Picture of pyramid in Egypt from the Internet
16 Intersection in Chicago, 2018 by Paul Preissner
17 Picture of building from the Internet
18 Picture of back of building from the Internet
19 Picture of bedroom from the Internet
20 Mars Chocolate North America, 2020 by Paul Preissner
21 Model of the moon from the Internet
22 Mars landscape, 2017 by Curiosity Rover, NASA
23 La Riviera Sports Bar and Disco, 2011 by Alex Lehnerer
24 Drawing of Hamburger Rathhausbau, 1876
25 Alfred R Preissner Company Car by Alfred Preissner
26 My parent's Buick Roadmaster interior, 2019 by Paul Preissner
27 Pool in Sheboygan, 2016 by Paul Preissner
28 Andrew Rafacz Gallery by Paul Preissner Architects, 2020 by Ian Vecchiotti
29 Grimsel Wanderweg Eingang Artilleriewerk, 2015 by Paul Preissner
30 "We lived in this apartment when I was younger, so there was still traces of when I lived in this room when I was 2 or 3 years old." 2017 by Adrien Blondel
31 Screaming Beatles fans from the Internet
32 Snoopy latte art from the Internet
33 "Turkey," 2019 by Amelia Preissner
34 Yeoui Naru Ferry Terminal, 2017 by Paul Preissner Architects
35 Some tree in England from the Internet
36 Sad face from the Internet
37 House rendering from the Internet
38 Robin Hood Hotel in Sheffield, UK from the Internet
39 "Mona Lisa," 2019 by Amelia Preissner
40 Sandwich, 2018 by Paul Preissner
41 Erlangen, 2019 by Paul Preissner
42 Mity Red Potatoes, 2016 by Paul Preissner
43 Fern plants from the Internet
44 Thin building from the Internet
45 Grands Ensembles immobiliers du Mail, 1960 by Ville de Vélizy
46 "This car that can go so fast and it can break anything," 2019 by August Preissner
47 Carpeted stairs from the Internet
48 Crossroads from Nowhere to Nowhere from the Internet
49 "Albany, from Van-Unsselaens Island." Engraving from The History and Topography of the United States of North America by John Howard Hinton (Boston, 1846). 30-N-36-322
50 The Executive Motor Hotel Richmond, Virginia, 1960's Vintage Postcard
51 Man at his desk in an office from the Internet
52 Mall interior from the Internet
53 Some abandoned construction project from the Internet
54 "Sea is for Cookie," 2014 by reddit user Put_It_All_On_Red
55 American Framing Pavilion Model, 2019 by Paul Andersen and Paul Preissner
56 Alfred R Preissner Plumbing storefront on Division Street, by Alfred Preissner
57 Flat Round Tables, 2015 by Paul Preissner Architects
58 Amelia's lost ice cream, 2014 by Paul Preissner
59 "A Colorful Bird," 2018 by August Preissner

60 Balloons lost at some kids activity center, 2017 by Paul Preissner
61 City County Building Plaza perspective, 2014 by Paul Andersen and Paul Preissner
62 Snow White without makeup, 2015 by Walt Disney Studios, Loryn Brantz/BuzzFeed
63 Cat-person from the Internet
64 Hamburg, Germany, 1904 by Hans Breuer
65 City County Building Plaza plan, 2014 by Paul Andersen and Paul Preissner
66 Department store display from the Internet
67 A very nice van from the Internet
68 Some street in Sheffield, UK from the Internet
69 Video store from the Internet
70 Garage plan from the Internet
71 "Paul Preissner," 2019 by Amelia Preissner
72 Raccoon on the side of the road from the Internet
73 Gravel yard from the Internet
74 Hair + Hair in Sheboygan, 2020 by Paul Preissner
75 A wig from the Internet
76 Building on North Cicero Avenue I think, 2020 by Paul Preissner
77 Toast monster, every week by Paul Preissner
78 Erlangen hotel art, 2019 by Paul Preissner
79 Belgorod development plan, 2013 by Paul Preissner Architects
80 "Painting of a car and a soldier car," 2019 by August Preissner
81 Sports field in desert from the Internet
82 Basement living room in a house for sale from the Internet
83 My Dad at a garden party, 1973 by my Mom
84 Me getting a ticket from a Texas State Trooper, 2011 by Alex Lehnerer
85 Bandai S.H.Figuarts *Ghostbusters* Marshmallow Man Action Figure, 2017

Acknowledgments

Kind of Boring would not exist without the enthusiasm, support, criticism, eyeballs, and inspiration of many people. I'm thankful to have lucked into working with and around so many creative, funny, and weird people.

I'd like to first thank those who made this book possible. Working with Ricardo Devesa and Actar has been a delightful process. Jayne Kelley, Tim Kinsella, Alex Lehnerer, Walter Benn Michaels, and Li Tavor—I'm humbled by your willingness to contribute; my opinions and outlooks would not be what they are without having first been a fan of your opinions and outlooks. I'm grateful to Courtney Coffman for all your criticisms, suggestions, edits and help in clearing up my uncombed thoughts. Joe Gilmore, working with you on this book has been a gift.

My debt to Bob Somol will be apparent to any reader. I'd still be making much different work if it wasn't for him and I'm grateful for the opportunity to acknowledge it here. Thanks also go to my friends across the School of Architecture; College of Architecture, Design, and the Arts; and Department of English at the University of Illinois at Chicago—I can not imagine a better intellectual home than the one we have here. I'd especially like to thank Paul Andersen for the invitation to work together on a barn, which has turned into much more. I don't have the vocabulary to properly express the thanks owed to Michael Speaks for his belief in what must have seemed like an incoherent twenty years of exploration.

I am forever appreciative to everyone who has given their time and assistance to the work within and not within this book: Paul Adjokun, Anton Bakerjian, Patrick Baudin, Ilija Bentscheff, Brandon Biederman, Evan Bliss, Jason Cave, Jason Chernak, Stephen Coorlas, Jesus Corral, Julia Di Castri, Hamish Dickson, John Dillon, Dana Elkhoury, Juliana Esposito, Rezvan Farahany, Martin Franks, Joanna Grant, Brett Gustafson, Ryan Hendryx, Ryan Hernandez, Ryan Johnson, Don Kalant, Jr., Vanessa Kokott, Chris Koster, Katie LaCourt, Nadia Lohse, Jared Macken, Marcella Martinez, Ian McHone, Jeff Mikolajewski, Katherine Monachos, David Mulder, Peter Overman, Dominic Peternel, Nick Poulos, Elnaz Rafati, David Ramis, Isabelle Redford, Rebekah Schaberg, Stanley Schultz, Agata Siemionow, Katherine Simson, Amelia Tabeling, Matt Utley, Matt van der Ploeg, Jacob Waas, Warren Weaver, and Michael Wolff.

Finally, I want to thank the people who have supported and suffered me the longest—without your friendships my world would be a much smaller and less fulfilling place. Mike Bray, Alan Froberg, and Matt Knox, I'd be adrift without our continuous conversations. Mack Hagood, what a wonderful surprise it was to become friends. I feel like we went from just meeting because of two dogs (RIP Lulu and Bamboo!) to becoming connected at the hip (through iMessage!). Steve Lamos, I cannot thank you enough for your model example and equally cynical outlook, and how weird is all of this, anyway!? Alex Lehnerer, we've been friends since we met (almost!), surviving oceans of distance, mountains, and even the Texas Highway Patrol! Fred Popolo, I've had the joy of creating, performing, and building work with you for decades. Chris Strong, I can't thank you enough for your eyeballs and observations. Julie Rodrigues Widholm, thank you for finding something interesting in this work before there was much evidence there was.

I'm fortunate to have married into the family that I did with Joan, Chris and Kim, and Mike. I'm very thankful to be a part of it. Mom and Dad, thank you for teaching me how to be curious and inquisitive and to find the value in being bored. Karl, we've been best friends for nearly my entire life and your understanding and companionship have made me a better person.

Cathleen, without your endless love, togetherness, and jokes this work would be nonexistent; thank you. This book is for Amelia and August—you have both profoundly changed me and I'll never be able to thank you enough.

Colophon

Kind of Boring: Canonical Work and Other Visible Things Meant to be Viewed as Architecture

Published by
Actar Publishers, New York, Barcelona
www.actar.com

Author
Paul Preissner

Edited by
Courtney Coffman

With contributions by
Jayne Kelley, Tim Kinsella, Alex Lehnerer, Walter Benn Michaels, Li Tavor

Copy editing and proofreading
Ideas on Fire

Graphic design
Joe Gilmore

Typefaces
Lÿno by Radim Peško
Favorit by Dinamo

Papers
Symbol Pearl
Symbol Freelife Gloss
Pop'Set Sweet Rose

Printing and binding
Arlequin, Barcelona

Distribution
Actar D, Inc. New York, Barcelona.

New York
440 Park Avenue South, 17th Floor
New York, NY 10016, USA
T +1 2129662207
salesnewyork@actar-d.com

Barcelona
Roca i Batlle 2-4
08023 Barcelona, Spain
T +34 933 282 183
eurosales@actar-d.com

Indexing
ISBN 978-1-948765-13-8
PCN: Library of Congress Control Number 2018964805

Publication date:
November 2020

46

G4

47

O5

06

CROSSROADS FROM NOWHERE TO NOWHERE

48

49

50

51

12

52

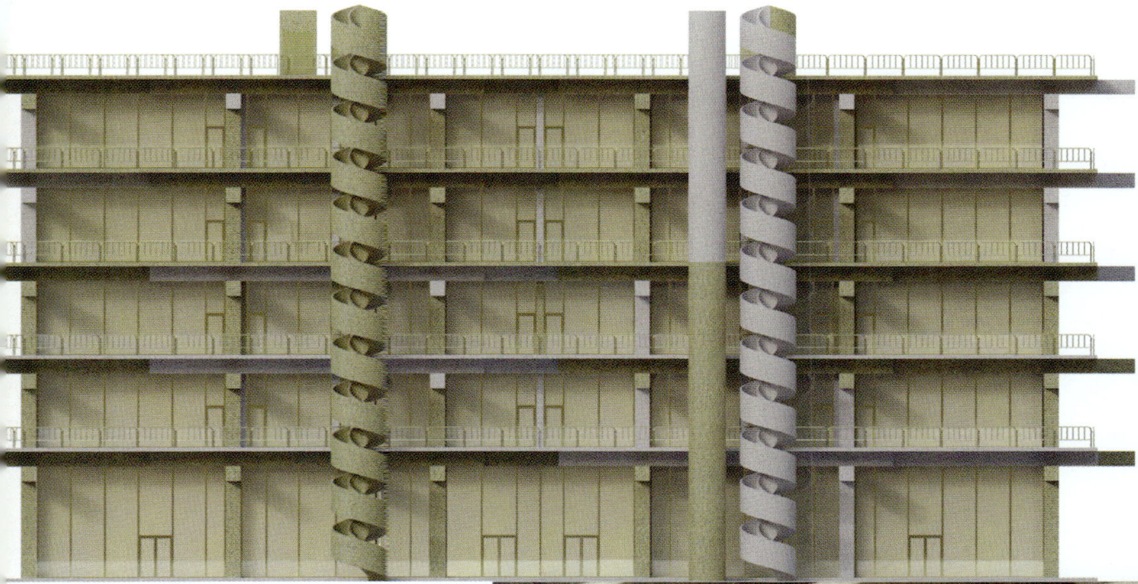

A4

53

54

1826

C8

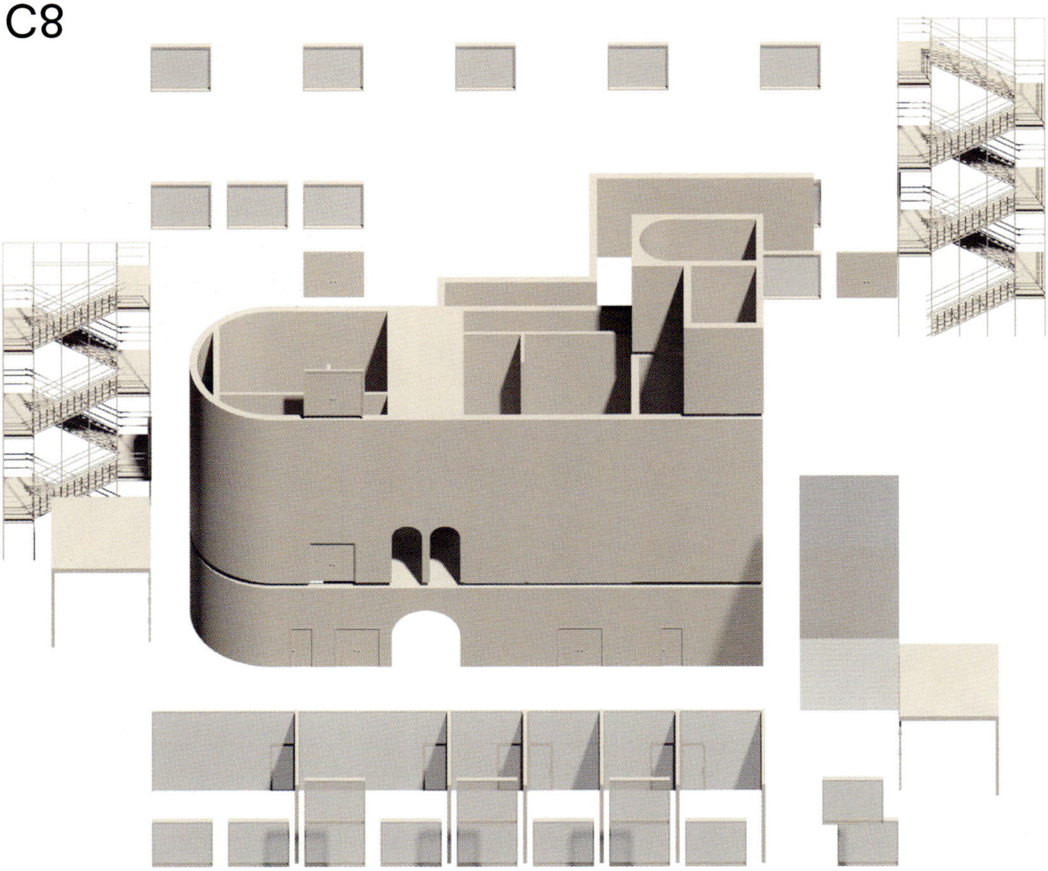

D1

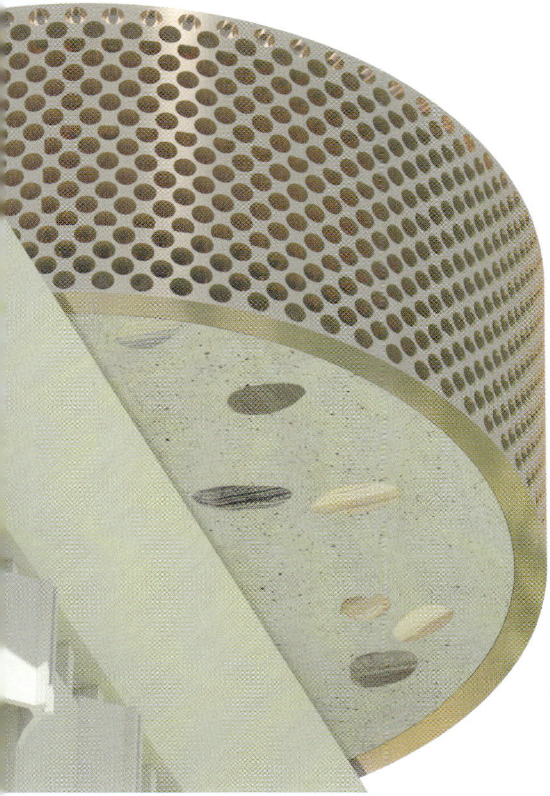

D2

55

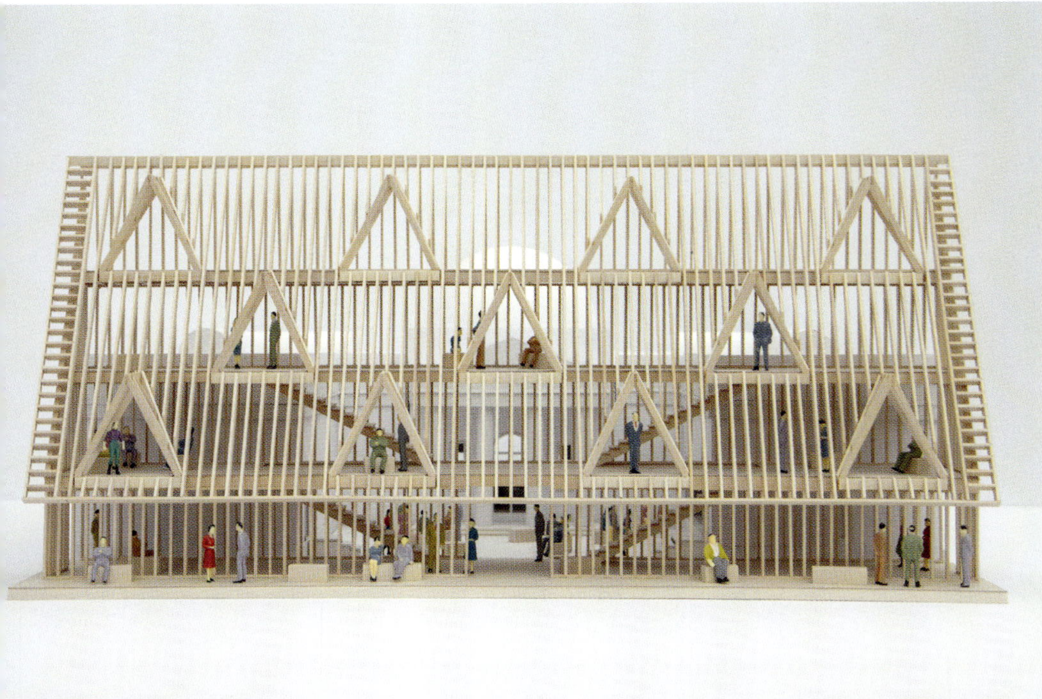

L6

C9

57

K8

58

E13

59

60

F7

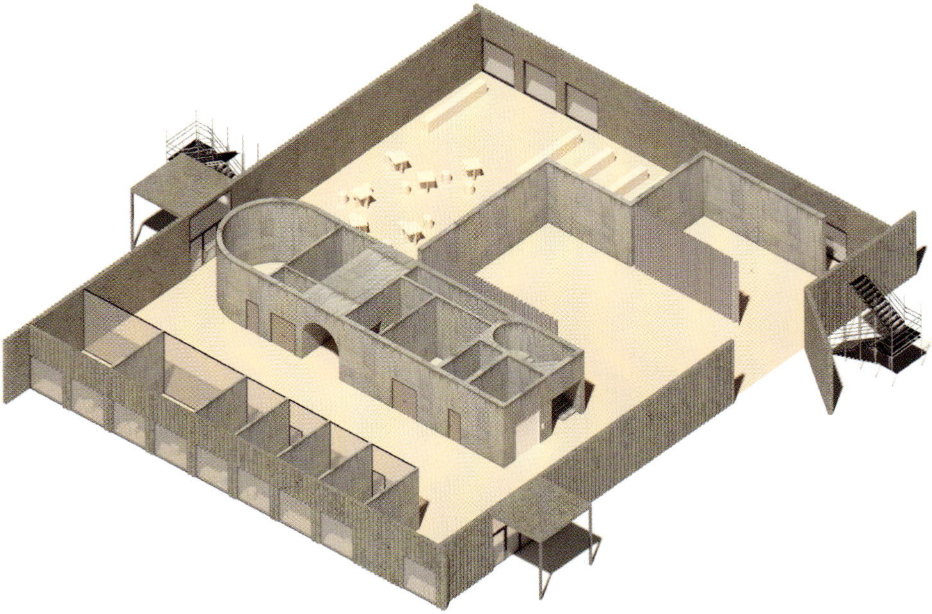

C10

F8

B2

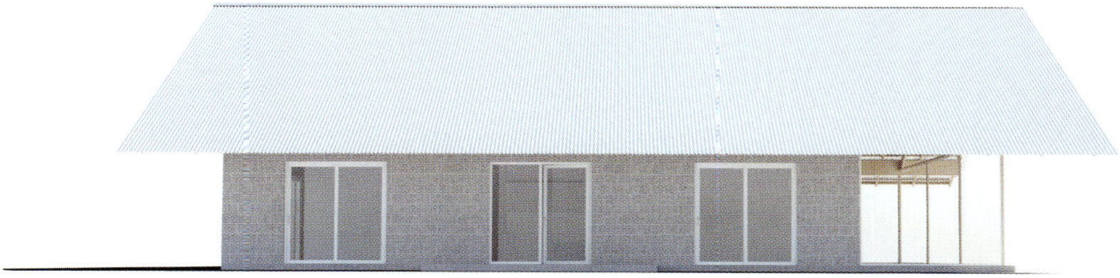

61

62

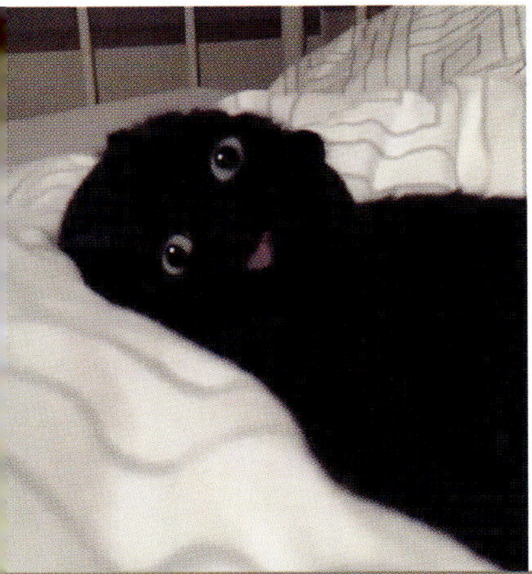

63

N5

C11

K9

L7

A6

64

65

F9

66

67

H1

220

68

E14

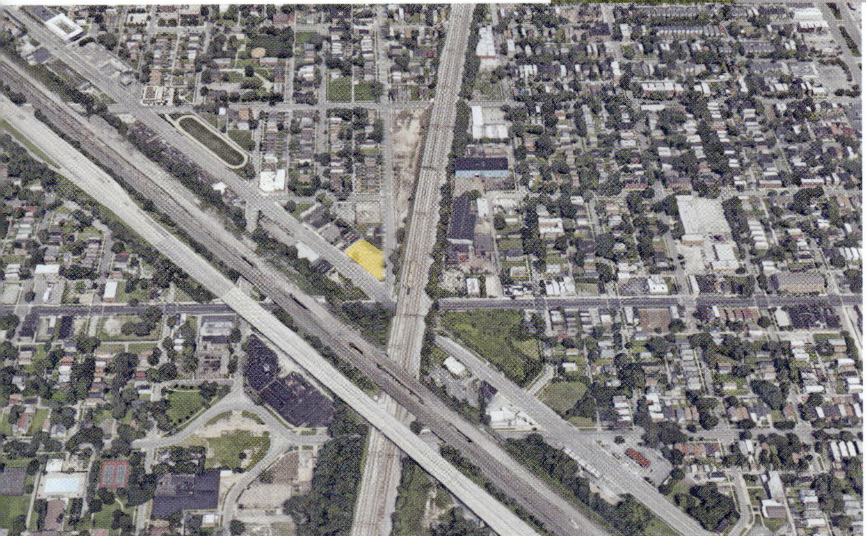

C12

69

70

71

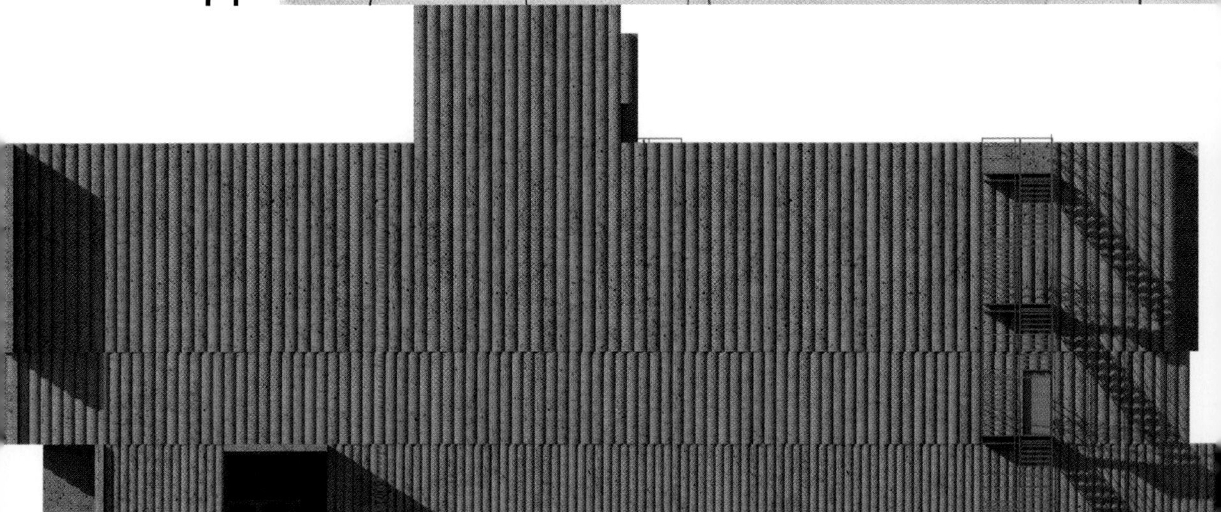

C13

72

K10

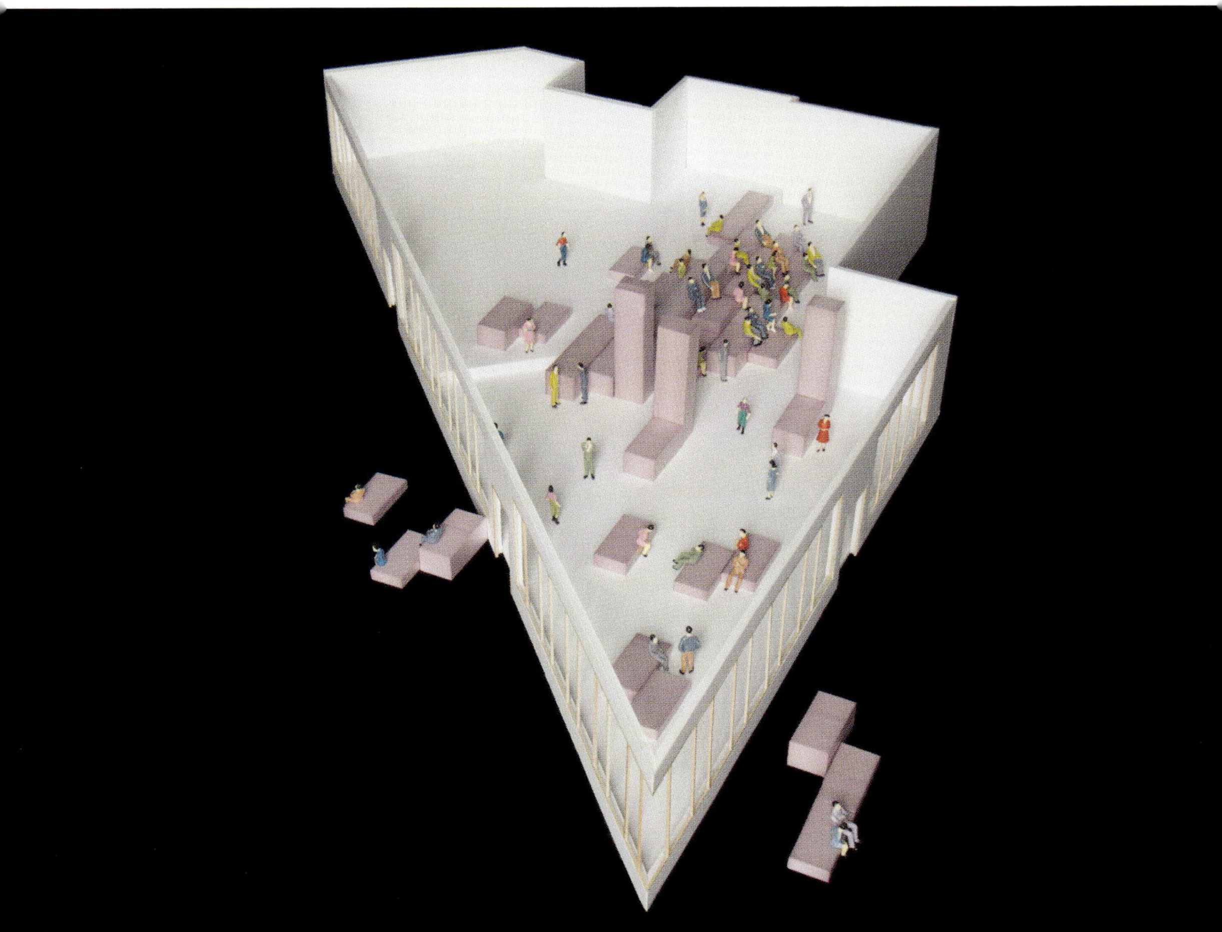

M6

73

A8

I3

Art
Complex

A10

74

75

D4

76

77

78

D5

79

80

 A11

B3

81

82

L10

83

244 84